In the last chapter of his book Dr. Okello succinctly juxtaposes the reasons for believers pain and suffering whil_____ h a lucid explanation of the happine  he writes that such eternal life will be _____ ed Christ as their redeemer and Lord _____ e joy set before them of glorious resur_____ . Okello offers a well reasoned, clear a_____ ____ ___ _or the Christian's belief in eternal life in heaven. This is an interesting, lively, informative, but spiritually challenging book. I wholeheartedly endorse it.

Rev. Dr. Joseph G. Njoroge
Professor of Political Science & Religion
Chair, Department of History & Political Science
Abraham Baldwin State College/University of Georgia System.
Chairman: Board of Trustees, Kenya Christian Fellowship in America.

Joseph Okello has offered a clear and concise explanation why heaven is a place of answered questions. He shows that heaven is an intelligent hope based on the history of salvation that culminated in Jesus' resurrection from the dead, and he shows that the questions surrounding our universe and why we are here can only be answered if a place like heaven exists. This is inspirational and informing!

Dr. Laurence W. Wood
Frank Paul Morris Professor of Systematic Theology/Wesley Studies
Asbury Theological Seminary

Here is a sound, biblically based book that engages our often asked questions about heaven in a profound yet down to earth way. Joseph Okello writes with a scholars mind and a pastor's heart. Read this book and be both better informed about our blessed future hope and inspired to live more faithfully and joyfully here and now.

Dr. Steve Seamands
Professor of Christian Doctrine
Asbury Theological Seminary

Heaven

God's Solution to Human Pain

Joseph B. Onyango Okello

WestBow
P R E S S

WestBow Press books may be ordered through booksellers or by contacting:

WestBow Press
A Division of Thomas Nelson
1663 Liberty Drive
Bloomington, IN 47403
www.westbowpress.com
1-(866) 928-1240

Because of the dynamic nature of the Internet, any Web addresses or links contained in this book may have changed since publication and may no longer be valid. The views expressed in this work are solely those of the author and do not necessarily reflect the views of the publisher, and the publisher hereby disclaims any responsibility for them.

ISBN: 978-1-4497-0319-6 (sc)
ISBN: 978-1-4497-0320-2 (hc)
ISBN: 978-1-4497-0318-9 (e)

Library of Congress Control Number: 2010931009

Unless otherwise indicated, all Bible passages are taken from The New International Version

Printed in the United States of America

WestBow Press rev. date: 6/29/2010

To:

Lila Hersey, Martha Warfield, Betty Davis, Mary Warfield, Lamont Washington, Ann Simpson, David Gichuru and David Stroh – who left the land of the dying and went to the land of the living.

Acknowledgements

The circumstances in which the idea for this book was birthed came innocently enough. Pastor Wendell Lewis, senior pastor of Jimtown Baptist Church, invited me to be the revival speaker at Jimtown Baptist Church's fall 2009 revival. As the week of revival drew close, I realized I had not quite settled on a possible revival topic. After continuous prayer and soul-searching, it became evident to me that I needed to explore the possibility of speaking about heaven. More specifically, I felt I needed to talk about the hope of heaven and its implications for our earthly lives.

At the end of the revival week, a number of those who attended the revival asked if they could get copies of the series of sermons for that week. Others advised me to put the sermons in print in order to reach a wider audience. I took up the challenge, and that led to the writing and completion of this book.

As I began to write, however, I found myself leaning toward a much narrower theme. That is, I felt that the goals of this book would be better served if I allowed the original series of sermons to morph into something more focused. For example, I felt I needed to focus more on how the hope of heaven could help us live through the sufferings and pains presented to us by our earthly lives. As I read and studied more, I settled on biblical passages that assured suffering Christians that all their sufferings will eventually come to an end.

I must therefore thank Pastor Wendell Lewis and members of Jimtown Baptist Church for having a vision that crystallized into the book you now hold in your hands. I would also like to thank members of Jimtown United Methodist Church for their support and encouragement. They have always created an environment conducive to the development and eventual completion of projects of this sort.

Students and faculty of Asbury Theological Seminary were equally supportive. I am very grateful for their comments and valuable criticisms. In particular, I would like to thank Steve Harper, James Miller, Steve Seamands, and Laurence Wood, all from Asbury

Seminary; Jones Kaleli from Liberty University; and Joseph Njoroge from Abraham Baldwin's State College. These professors read different chapters of this book and provided insightful comments and suggestions for improvement. Any shortcomings that might attend this book are of course my own.

My wife Sophie has also given me unrivaled support, second only to what Christ gives. I will therefore be forever grateful to her. Lastly, I give praise, honor and glory to our Lord and Savior Jesus Christ, without whom the hope of heaven would always be an illusion.

Contents

I. Introduction

One of the most fascinating themes of Christian theology is the doctrine of heaven. For centuries humans have tried to determine whether their souls can and do survive after death. Many answers have been given, some assuring us that there indeed exists a place called heaven, while others contend that the deaths of our loved ones basically signify the end of our relationships with them, and that we have no hope of ever seeing them again. Serious Christians who rest their hope in living eternally after death will of course find the second answer unpalatable. This is because it seems to run contrary to what they believe Scripture teaches.

It is not my intention in this book to argue for the existence of heaven.[1] I believe that this task has been accomplished by more capable thinkers and theologians. Rather, on the assumption that heaven is indeed a real place in which believers in Christ's saving grace will find themselves, I try to show how the reality of the doctrine of heaven functions as a satisfactory solution to the problem of suffering – a problem faced by both believers and unbelievers alike. I contend, however, that only believers will have the privilege of enjoying the promise of heaven.

---

1   However, toward the end of this book I draw attention to various reasons that
      Christian thinkers give for believing that heaven exists.

I have deliberately chosen to avoid scholarly language in this work for very simple reasons. First, pieces of scholarly work on heaven are already available. Hence those who wish to look at a much deeper treatment of heaven can always peruse those works. Second, the writing of this book was inspired by a series of sermons that I preached in a three-day revival service at Jimtown Baptist Church, Lexington, Kentucky. After receiving a lot of encouragement from those who attended the services there, I felt it would be a pity to pass up the opportunity to present the material on the printed page. In order to make the material as accessible as the Jimtown sermons were, I decided to make this work simple and understandable.

For this reason, those familiar with my two previous works will quickly find the language in this book relatively simple and, hopefully, straightforward. Of course this might be a disappointment to those who perhaps hoped for a more academic treatment of the subject. However, the aim of this book is strictly pastoral rather than academic. In order to reach his flock, the pastor must do his best to execute the responsibilities of his calling in as down-to-earth a manner as possible. This is especially true for suffering parishioners who desire simple and uncomplicated answers for why they suffer as they do.[2] To be sure, many philosophers of religion agree that the suffering Christian will perhaps not be helped by sophisticated philosophical arguments detailing why a good, loving and just God allows his children to suffer. What the suffering Christian really needs is the sort of pastoral care that assures him or her that God can still be trusted even in the midst of tragedy.

Like most believers, I have been unfortunate enough to watch loved ones suffer. The fact that I am a pastor did not make this experience any easier for me. I have struggled and continue to struggle through the process with suffering parishioners. Like any pastor, I have made numerous hospital visitations to pray with suffering parishioners faced with the uncertainties that their situations seemed

---

2   By asserting this, however, I do not say that this book gives us the solution to the problem of suffering. This book is merely a pointer to the solution. The solution for the problem of suffering will be made available to all of God's children in heaven, which is the overall thesis of this book.

to entail for them. In such instances, I have been forced to give them a shoulder to cry on, or at least be at the forefront in doing so. At other times I have only watched helplessly as they asked the all too important why-question concerning their suffering. This is especially so in cases where loved ones died unexpectedly, tragically snatched from their significant others by some unexpected event.

Whereas the answer and solutions to such questions and situations are perhaps not immediately available, this does not imply that they will never be available at all. The purpose of this book is to assure believers that in the long run, our sufferings will be taken away, if the promise of heaven is anything to go by. Hence, if this book is to fully address the problem of suffering for Christians across the board, whether in a scholarly or a non-scholarly fashion, the language must also be accessible to all.

However, in spite of taking this direction, I still caution the reader that a very minute section of the information presented in the book will be engaging in some respects. I refer, for example, to the sixth chapter wherein I try to show how the experience of heaven will be one in which all our unanswered questions in this life will finally be settled. Just the same, a slow pace of reading and reflection on the issues should help the reader to clarify the information for him- or herself. We are dealing here with deep concepts, some of which will require both diligence and determination to understand the material.

Having said this, I must also present a disclaimer. I do not purport to be an authority on the topic of heaven. What I present here are the findings I have made during my personal readings of portions of Scripture addressing the subject. The study was motivated by attempts to encourage suffering believers to "hang in there" as they struggled through their pains. For this reason, it is quite possible that those more versed with the discipline of biblical interpretation will perhaps find my exegesis somewhat suspect. I humbly submit my ignorance here, in the hope that I will be corrected.

Also, whereas this work is meant to help the believer think for himself or herself when considering the verses of Scripture cited here, I urge the believer to adopt a standpoint of cross-checking the

Scriptural references to make sure that what I think it says is really what it says. It might just be, from the reader's standpoint, that what I think the text in question says is perhaps misleading. To such an individual, I once again humbly submit my ignorance, hoping that his or her correction will be forthcoming.

This is essentially a pastoral book. It seeks to help the parishioner through his or her struggles with tragedy. The aim is to help the believer somehow find meaning in suffering. The assumption, of course, is that there *is* meaning in suffering. Sometimes we do locate meaning in pain. Sometimes, however, we are hard pressed to find one. My contention is that such meaning, though sometimes invisible here on earth, will definitely be locatable in heaven.

I also contend that the alternative offered by the unbelieving atheistic vantage point is really not feasible at all. It is an alternative that admits that the universe has no meaning, and that our pains and tragedies are therefore meaningless. Such a situation is absolutely hopeless, and practically unlivable. The Christian believer need not subscribe to this world-view, for it offers no motivation for living. However, the knowledge that there is purpose in suffering, in spite of the fact that such suffering came, initially, through the fall of human beings in the Garden of Eden, enables us as believers to live our lives with full assurance that everything will be made right by God. This is a hope that no one else can give except the one who put the foundations of this universe in place. Allow me to give a brief synopsis below on how this book is structured.

In the second chapter I focus on the theme of greatness. I note, for example, that heaven is a place of greatness. This is evidenced by the greatness of the city, that is, the New Jerusalem; by the greatness of the citizens of heaven; and finally, by the greatness of God. To underscore the greatness of the city, I compare its size and dimensions with earthly cities. It immediately becomes clear that cities with human hands are non-starters compared with the heavenly city. I do note, however, that perhaps the author of Revelation was not in any way giving us literal dimensions of the city. Just the same, if we were to take its size literally, we discover at once how dismally small our earthly cities turn out in comparison. Also, I try to capture the Scriptural portrayals of the greatness of the citizens of heaven. I then draw attention to the greatness of God, admitting that God's greatness cannot really be captured in human language. His greatness is such that to express it in words is really an exercise in futility; for by doing so one really does injustice to the notion of God's greatness. I then point to verses of Scripture that allude to God's greatness, and draw possible implications from them.

In the third chapter I focus on the beauty of heaven. Once again, drawing from Scripture, I try my best to paint a picture of beauty that only the hope of heaven can give. As with the second chapter, I begin with the beauty of the city of heaven, with the aim of drawing comparisons between the beauty of earthly cities and the beauty of the New Jerusalem. Once again, from Scripture, I conclude that the beauty of earthly cities cannot be compared with that of the New Jerusalem. I also note that since Christians will be glorified in heaven, we must assume that the transformation captured by this glorification will be the most beautiful transformation any human being will ever live through. Moreover, I contend, as I did with God's greatness, that God's beauty is indescribable in human language. Once we set eyes on him, we will be awed by what we will see. We will also be delighted to discover that in heaven, God will give himself to us in all such beauty so we can enjoy our eternal relationship of holy and pure love with him forever.

In the fourth chapter I turn to the question of healing. Noting that all humans will suffer at one time or another in their lives, heaven is the place in which true healing will take place. In this chapter, I turn to passages of Scripture that speak about healing in heaven. I do so in order to help illustrate the anticipated reality of just this healing. I note, for example, that human beings will find healing from physical suffering as well as from emotional suffering. I also note that the created order will be healed as well. The implication of all these experiences of healing is the truth depicted by the promise that God will wipe away all our tears, for the old order of things will have passed away. This is perhaps one of the more significant chapters of this work, since it speaks about heaven in a way that directly relates to our physical instances of suffering.

Holiness is the subject of the fifth chapter. Here, I focus on the holiness of the city in a way analogous to my focus on its beauty and greatness. I also focus on the holiness of the citizens of the city, as well as on the holiness of God. The contention is simply this: heaven is a holy place. For this reason, nothing unholy will enter heaven. Closely tied to God's holiness is the idea of God's justice. Since God is holy, he will not let unholy and unrepentant people (murderers, liars, adulterers, rapists and the like) enter his holy abode. Only those who allow the blood of Christ to cleanse them from sin will enter heaven. I do my best to depict God as holy, but I do so with fear and trembling, lest my description fails to do justice to what God's holiness truly looks like.

I also note that most of the questions we have asked here on earth will have answers in heaven. This is the subject of the sixth chapter. I contend in that chapter that heaven will provide answers to questions hitherto unanswered. Besides the question of suffering, I note that heaven will also answer five of some of the most fundamental questions that we all tend to ask, questions that great thinkers and ordinary persons have thought about and categorized as those of origin, morality, meaning, identity and destiny. I show that only heaven will truly reveal how God, and our relationship with him, will provide answers that fully and most completely addresses these concerns.

In the seventh chapter, I focus on the question of abundant life. Having my focus on Christ's eternally true claim that he is the giver of abundant life, I observe that only in heaven will this truth be most evident. After expounding on this issue, I conclude by arguing that there exists nothing we consider good here on earth for which heaven does not have an infinitely superior alternative. Only in heaven will we find pleasure, happiness, joy, satisfaction and contentment and the like in their purest, holiest and highest form. It is a destiny that no sensible person should pass up. It is a destiny that all believers should seek to enjoy. Hence, the person who passes up God's offer for salvation really puts him- or herself at the pitiful risk of missing out on God's greatest offer to humankind.

I then conclude, in the eighth chapter, by suggesting that the hope of heaven has various implications for our lives here on earth. More specifically, I contend that the hope of heaven enables us to find meaning in our earthly lives in everything we do. If this is indeed the case, then our visit to the mall or to the grocery store is just as meaningful to us, for example, as our worship experience in God's temple; for we are constantly aware that God made us for a purpose, and that anything we do revolves around our relationship with him. In addition, we discover that all our experiences, whether those involving moments of intense suffering, or those less severe, serve to fulfill just those very purposes for which God made us. Put differently, whatever happens to us turn out to be the sorts of experiences that did not take God by surprise. He was fully aware of their happenings before they came to be. In order to explore all these more fully, let's begin with the first motif, namely: heaven is a place of greatness.

II. Heaven is a Place of Greatness

Half-way through my primary education, I vowed to remain undyingly focused in my pursuit of fame and fortune. The desire to be great overwhelmed me. I was ready to stop at nothing until I got what I desired. Quite frankly, I neither knew what that meant nor understood the demands a pursuit of this nature would later make on me. Nevertheless, like any ambitious young person, I wanted to be some great doctor, perhaps famous for inventing something like a hoped-for treatment for cancer or AIDS. If it should eventually turn out that I did not succeed in being a doctor, plan B was well situated – I wanted to be a pilot or an engineer of some kind.

However, as I made my progress through primary school, and later through high school, a quick glance at my grades portrayed something different. I was not doing well. My progress report card was anything but progress. I started off very well in high school, but gradually yielded my rank almost to the bottom of the class, much to my parents' consternation. If I was planning to be a great person, I was clearly not treading on that road. I had to do something about my academic performances.

At the end of my high-school education, I did not score enough points to grant me entry into any of the state universities. I remember walking home with the result slip in my hands. My father was in his bedroom, down with a fever. He was not doing too well, so I felt reluctant to disclose to him the results of my poor performance. Why add the pain of my failure to his misery? When I walked into his bedroom, though, he insisted on wanting to know how I performed in my final exams. Upon disclosing the information to him, his response surprised me. I expected a violent outburst of emotions, including verbal pyrotechnics of some kind. Instead he assured me that someday I would make it to the highest level of education in whatever area God would choose for me. Little did I know how prophetic that assurance would eventually turn out, and the blessing that came along with it.

My father's words still ring in my ears. How could he speak with such clarity and confidence about my future even when the evidence that lay before him on that day pointed to something stark, bereft of promise? To this day I will not be able to account for his confidence in the midst of such despair except to suggest that his deep faith in God allowed him to utter these words. He never lived to see me graduate, either from college, from graduate school or from post-graduate school. Oddly, he anticipated all these even after I had gradually lost hope in their possible fulfillment.

My ambition to be great was never realized. If anything I abandoned it after responding to what I now believe was God's call on my heart. I no longer have it as my goal; for after years of theological and philosophical education, I have discovered that when one is a believer in Jesus Christ, one need not worry about greatness. In fact it seems to be the case that the more we pursue greatness, as defined by the world, the more it eludes us. Perhaps one should abandon all attempts to be great in this way.

What I find interesting, however, is the following fact: according to Scripture, our Lord Jesus Christ has carved a path to greatness for every believer. It is a path that may not be realized in this lifetime. To be sure, in some cases, the path to greatness may require that the unbeliever should pass through numerous instances of humiliation and suffering in this lifetime. This is true of many Christians around the world facing persecution on a daily basis. It is true of many believers for whom three meals per day is a luxury beyond their reach. It is true of believers subjected to servitude, slavery and human trafficking.

In spite of such realities and their severity, greatness is guaranteed for every believer. True greatness will not be achieved in this life. In fact, true greatness *cannot* be achieved in this life; for the certainty of death will surely take any self-induced forms of human invincibility. True greatness, Scripture tells us, is available for the believer in Jesus Christ once we enter heaven. Moreover, this greatness is not the sort of greatness that ends in death as is the case with earthly forms of greatness. The greatness in question is eternal greatness – one that will never come to an end, one that every believer will enjoy.

This should, in ways that I will explain below, provide some hope for suffering Christians, enabling them to deal with their pain. Without question, many believers face instances of severe trials, some of them deeply horrendous. As one with pastoral experience in churches in the West and in Africa, I can quite confidently say that suffering is no respecter of persons. All human beings will suffer at some stage in their lives, and the Christian is of no exception. I have stood by the bedside of believers dying of painful terminal illnesses, and watched as life ebbed slowly from their bodies. I have buried dear friends in both continents, while at the same time having to deal with the despair that has come to so much characterize their daily lives. I have been shocked by the brutal report of close friends cruelly, brutally and suddenly taken away by death. Moreover, the frequencies with which such events occur seem to intensify with the passage of time.

With such personal experiences bedeviling believers, it is quite easy to throw in the towel and give up on life, on friends and on God. As apologist Ravi Zacharias correctly notes, when an individual turns away from God in such instances, we must ask: to what or to whom will that individual turn? By contrast, the believer who knows his Bible and knows the promises that lie ahead need not fall for the logic that urges us to turn away from God when life becomes difficult, as rigorous as that logic may seem to be.

For example, using this very logic unbelieving philosophers have tried to coax believers into thinking that there cannot be a good and loving God who allows his children to go through the sorts of trials and pain with which we have now become familiar. Without undermining the seriousness of their charge (but almost at the risk of doing so) is it not fair to observe that such objections to God's existence are quite misleading for many reasons?

One such reason is that they make quick judgments about God based on only a fraction of one's life, namely, this life. They forget that for the Christian, there is a whole lifetime of eternity that must be brought into consideration as well. If, after death, the Christian is meant to enjoy a life of greatness and happiness with God for all eternity, then even a lifetime of pain on this earth will surely not be sufficient to make the believer renounce his God. In Romans 8:18-21 The Apostle Paul places his finger on this very issue as he penned the following words through the inspiration of the Holy Spirit. He writes:

> I consider that our present sufferings are not worth comparing with the glory that will be revealed in us. The creation waits in eager expectation for the sons of God to be revealed. For the creation was subjected to frustration, not by its own choice, but by the will of the one who subjected it, in hope that the creation itself will be liberated from its bondage to decay and brought into the glorious freedom of the children of God.

If an earthly lifetime of pain is what it will take to enjoy eternal life, then so be it. Many Christians have gladly walked down that road; for they know that what awaits them is indescribably and incomparably great. That is not to say that such believers take their suffering lightly. On the contrary, they take their suffering most seriously. They "groan inwardly" so to speak. The reason they cannot think of abandoning God or turning away from him is precisely because they know that their deliverance from pain and suffering is on its way. In spite of the humiliation they have received from their suffering, a life of hope and greatness is on its way on the other side of death. It is this greatness that I will attempt to crystallize in the next few lines, though I must admit that I will not do a comprehensive job at it.

But exactly what sort of greatness are we talking about here? That very term has at least two facets. It is possible that there are more of these. For our purposes, however, I narrow them down to two. First,

Scripture seems to talk about greatness in terms of size. Second, it also talks about greatness in terms of social status. Indeed, the latter form of greatness seems to apply to every Christian believer, as we shall later see from the words of the Apostle Paul.

In light of these, let us explore three areas in which the redeemed believer in Jesus Christ will enjoy eternal greatness. First, heaven's capital city, the New Jerusalem, will be great in size. Second, the redeemed saint will be great in social status. Third, and most importantly, God will present himself to us as the Greatest Possible Being.

A. Heaven's Capital City Will Be Great

Two key passages, Revelation 21:9, 10 and Revelation 21:15-17 give us an idea of just how great heaven will be. They read as follows:

> One of the seven angels who had the seven bowls full of the seven last plagues came and said to me, "Come, and I will show you the bride, the wife of the Lamb. And he carried me away in the Spirit to a mountain great and high, and showed me the Holy City, Jerusalem, coming down out of heaven from God.

> The angel who talked with me had a measuring rod of gold to measure the city, its gates and its walls. The city was laid out like a square, as long as it was wide. He measured the city with the rod and found it to be 12,000 stadia in length, and as wide and high as it is long. He measured its wall and it was 144 cubits thick by man's measurement, which the angel was using.

There are interesting suggestions as to how we should interpret these passages, and the book of Revelation as a whole. This is specifically because compared to other books of Scripture the book has many instances of symbolic language, metaphors, strange characters and beasts – all of them foreign to the imagination especially of the Western mind. If we are to take these specifications and measurements literally, we are looking at an enormous city indeed. Even if we are to take them symbolically or metaphorically,

I doubt that we can escape its enormity. To a non-westerner like me, most of the book of Revelation presents little interpretive problems, much less this very passage whose measurements are quite clearly stipulated. Hence I will not worry too much about the interpretive procedure here, except to stay true to the language that presents itself to me.

Having said that, notice just how great, in terms of size, this city will be. It is cubicle in shape. Its length is twelve thousand stadia, which translates to approximately fourteen hundred miles. Its width is also about fourteen hundred miles. Likewise, it rises about fourteen hundred miles in height. I tried to calculate the space that the city will occupy. Since I used a calculator that I bought from a dollar store, the product of my calculation was too large to fit in the viewing screen! Nevertheless, when I used my scientific calculator, the volume of the city was 2744000000 cubic miles. That is an enormously large city.

Using earthly terms to describe this city, allow me to compare it with the current size of the city of New York. I take it that no building in New York, at least in the twenty-first century, is a mile tall. Hence if we try to calculate how many times New York would fit into heaven's capital city, it turns out to be over eight-hundred and ninety million times!

If we are to take these dimensions literally, some speculations about the city's greatness will be in order here. According to the biblical data, this is a city whose design will be sturdy, its dimensions will be accurate, its boundaries well-defined, its size unrivaled. Possible rivals will be clear non-starters. They pale in comparison – for no one can outdo the Master Architect in designing anything, leave alone a city of such proportions. I know of no creature with the sort of materials needed to design such a city. Such materials would not only be unavailable; they would also have to be enormously sturdy even to have the capacity for holding each other together without fissures developing or parts beginning to crumble.

Think about it this way: most of the buildings constructed by humans usually last for a specific period of time. Thereafter they either crumble to dust or get condemned as unfit for habitation. We have seen television footages of stadiums, casinos and skyscrapers brought down, in most cases, quite intentionally. The question to ask here, then, is this: why put up such constructions only to bring them down several years later? One major reason can be captured as follows: we feel that what we currently have is inadequate or defective. In other words, we wish to build something better to replace the less than perfect buildings we see. So in either case, we admit that what we wish to bring down is not as great as we would have liked it to be.

By contrast, notice how different heaven's capital city is. Unlike cities built by human hands, there will be no corrections to that city. It will have no demolitions. Not a single structure will ever be condemned, for the greatness of that city is eternal, enduring forever. Its foundation will never be shaken. No tsunamis will rock it. No earthquakes will bring its walls down. No hurricanes will flood its streets. No tornadoes will destroy its roofs. Thankfully, tsunamis, earthquakes, hurricanes and tornadoes will not even be there in the first place, for they are processes belonging quite properly to a fallen world and heaven, so we are reminded, will be a place of complete redemption from all sorts of fallenness. Thus we have a city not built by human hands, but tailor-made by God for every believer in Jesus Christ.

At this point we must ask: what does the greatness of that heavenly city mean for the believer in Jesus Christ? Somewhere in the heart of that city, the Lord Jesus Christ is preparing a room for his followers. Recall his words in John 14:1-4:

> Do not let your hearts be troubled. Trust in God, trust also in me. In my Father's house are many rooms; if it were not so, I would have told you. I am going to prepare a place for you. And if I go and prepare a place for you, I will come back and take you to be with me that you also may be where I am. You know the way where I am going.

The believer in Jesus Christ, redeemed by his precious blood, will definitely be a citizen of heaven. When you, as a believer in Christ, finally land there, one of the first things to visually present itself to you will be the greatness of the city itself. Another thing that will definitely impress itself upon you will be the greatness of your dwelling place. Every believer has been promised a dwelling place in that city. Strangely pleasant is the fact that there will be so much room and space in that city that there will be no homeless individuals there; for there will be enough space for everyone. Thus, when the image of heaven so presented is compared to our world, our cities and our homes, we really have no option but to conclude that the future comes with great promise for the believer.

I have lived in places considered, by the inhabitants of those places, anything but great. I have lived in a house whose only source of energy was a kerosene lamp, which sometimes emitted choking eye-burning smoke. I have lived in a house that had no running water, with the toilet facilities built separately from the house for obvious sanitary reasons. When I think of this city, I have no option but to have hope that everything will turn out alright for me as a believer in Christ

That is why believers living in unsanitary conditions through no fault of their own need to be encouraged that the unfortunate situation in which they find themselves will not last very long. For some believers, strong sturdy housing is a great need – an unaffordable luxury. They need not worry. Jesus is busy preparing a dwelling place for each and every one of them, one that will never be condemned; one that will always be a joy to live in; one that will engender a sense of holy pride; and one that will definitely press home the point that the believer has been a child of the king all along, a prince of a very real sort, so to speak. That is how great the capital city of heaven will be. There is more.

B. Heaven's Citizens Will be Great

It is not simply the case that our holy city in heaven will be great. It is also the case that the citizens of heaven, those redeemed by the blood of Christ, will also be great. As I write the introduction of this section, a very close friend of mine, David Stroh,[3] is gravely ill. We

---

3   This story is used with full permission from Judy Stroh, David's widow.

expect him to pass on to glory before this manuscript is over.[4] David was one of the first people I met when I set foot on American soil. The meeting was made possible through his son in law, Pastor Jeff Cartwright, whom I first met in seminary. We became great friends and have been friends since then. To say that David was a saint is quite possibly an understatement. He had a passion for God and for ministry. He served the Lord Jesus Christ with such conviction under the leadership of Pastor Jeff Cartwright. Whenever my wife and I travelled to Dayton, Ohio, to visit David, he would always invite us to sing in the choir, which he directed.

David's illness came about as surprisingly as any unexpected event. I was back in Kentucky, on my way home from a workout at the local gymnasium in Lexington, Kentucky. As I approached the first of the final intersections that would eventually lead me to my driveway, my cell phone rang. I could tell by looking at the caller ID that my friend Jeff was calling me. Assuming he was calling to inform me about my speaking engagement in that year's Christmas Eve service in his church, I delightedly picked up the phone and addressed him by his full name. He did not sound as enthusiastic. His words were terse and somber. "David Stroh had a heart attack," he said, "and we will appreciate it if you can keep him in your prayers."

For the next ten days we spent our devotional hours in agonizing prayer for David, asking the Lord to allow him to live on. As Christmas approached, it was becoming evident that David would perhaps not make it. When my wife and I finally arrived in Dayton, we discovered that the situation was worse than we had imagined. Upon entering David's room in the hospital, the tubes and gadgets, which the doctors stuck into his mouth, arms and fingers, told the whole story. David was dying – a fact too difficult to accept.

Several minutes later, David's wife Judy and their daughter Sharon Cartwright showed up. They were somber yet calm. After speaking with Judy and Sharon, they were both confident that David was in God's hands. Both of them epitomized the meaning of "allowing the powerful truths of the promise of heaven to come

---

4   David passed away thirty minutes after New Year's Day, January 1 2010.

alive in their lives." They knew that as much as David suffered here on earth, he was on a majestic road to Glory – the sort of Glory that no earthly human eyes have beheld since the Apostle John.

At this point, David's breathing is labored as he lies in bed under hospice care. His family is sitting around him waiting anxiously for that moment that he will be ushered into glory. They are sorrowful, yet joyful; sorrowful because they are about to say their final goodbyes and joyful because they know that what David is leaving behind pales in comparison to the beauty and majesty of his eternal home.

I use this story not only because I am about to say goodbye to a dear friend, but also because heaven is about to welcome home a fine citizen. To see and hear how his youngest son John recollects some of the humorous experiences the family had with their loved one, to watch how Steve calmly sits next to his mother with the assuring arms that only the eldest son can give at such trying times, and to watch Chuck, as they call him, respond to John's humor with grace, all leave me to conclude that David succeeded in raising a wonderful family.

Back in my home country, a bumper-sticker reminded me that a man's success is not evidenced by the money he has made, but by the family he has raised. Quite frankly, I do not know the origin of this statement. It could very well have originated from the West. However, it crystallizes a truth almost forgotten in a world bombarded with moral relativism and the so-called political correctness.

David's success, however, is seen in the family he has raised. All his children are believers, with wonderful spouses raising wonderful children. His success is further seen in the sort of life he lived, both as a respectable citizen and a born-again believer in the saving grace of our Lord Jesus Christ. This is the kind of citizen about to pass on to glory. The joy of it all is encapsulated by the fact that many more like him have gone on before him. It is quite likely that by the time you read this story, heaven will be celebrating David's arrival.

This leads me to what I wish to underscore in this chapter. Not only will heaven have a great capital city. It will also have great citizens. The most obvious citizen of heaven, of course, is God – to use human terms. There will be other citizens as well – angels and those of us redeemed by the blood of Jesus. I will focus more on human citizens in this section for two reasons. First, God's greatness needs a separate treatment in a different section owing to its enormity as a subject. Second, it is common knowledge among Christian believers that angels are quite superior in power and intellect, hence their greatness is not in doubt. What is doubtful, however, is whether human beings are the sort of creatures whose heavenly status will be somewhat promoted to a level that could quite properly be deemed great. I believe this will be the case. Several wonderful texts can be cited in support of this claim. Consider first, the words of Jesus in Matthew 13:41-43:

> The Son of Man will send out his angels, and they will weed out of his kingdom everything that causes sin and all who do evil. They will throw them into the fiery furnace, where there will be weeping and gnashing of teeth. Then the righteous will shine like the sun in the kingdom of their Father. He who has ears, let him hear.

Notice the contrast Jesus draws between the citizens of hell and the citizens of heaven. While the citizens of hell are burning, the citizens of heaven will be "shining like the sun in the kingdom of their Father." Something about their countenance will change for the better. It is fair to say that every believer will be shining just like God, as depicted in Revelation, will also be shining, though definitely in a much brighter way than the believer. I suspect this is what the Apostle John meant when he wrote the following: "Dear friends, now we are children of God, and what we will be has not yet been made known. But we know that when he appears, we shall be like him, for we shall see him as he is. Everyone who has this hope purifies himself, just as he is pure."[5] So, the countenance of the believers will definitely be great, as evidenced by the promise that they will shine like the stars.

Believers will not only be great in appearance; they will also be great as far as their social status is concerned. One of the most powerful passages illustrating how great the believer will be appears

---

5   I John 3:2

in 1 Corinthians 6:2-3, as follows: "Do you not know that saints will judge the world? And if you are to judge the world, are you not competent to judge trivial cases? Do you not know that we will judge angels? How much more the things of this life!" In another passage Paul writes: "If we endure, we will also reign with him ..." (2 Timothy 2:12). From the Pauline Epistles, therefore, we learn that our greatness as believers will be underscored by the fact that we will not only judge the world, we will also judge angels – quite possibly fallen angels. Also, the fact that we will reign with Christ is underscored. All these are instances of the greatness of status that believers will enjoy. Presumably, this is the sort of greatness that comes without the sin of pride that normally accompanies such dispositions.

The Apostle Paul was actually echoing Matthew 23:19 where Jesus says: "I tell you the truth, at the renewal of all things, when the Son of Man sits on his glorious throne, you who have followed me will also sit on twelve thrones, judging the twelve tribes of Israel." The word for judging in this passage, however, is more correctly understood as "ruling" or "governing." At any rate, the issue of greatness is underscored.

A much more significant indication of greatness is found in Revelation 20:4-6. It reads:

> I saw thrones on which were seated those who had been given authority to judge. And I saw the souls of those who had been beheaded because of their testimony for Jesus and because of the word of God. They had not worshiped the beast or his image and had not received his mark on their foreheads or their hands. They came to life and reigned with Christ a thousand years. (The rest of the dead did not come to life until the thousand years were ended.) This is the first resurrection. Blessed and holy are those who have part in the first resurrection. The second death has no power over them, but they will be priests of God and of Christ and will reign with him for a thousand years.

The interesting bit about this passage is that it has been given numerous interpretations by different schools of thought. However, the events in question here seem to happen before the arrival of the New Jerusalem, God's capital city. The believer's greatness is underscored, indicating that our promotion, as believers, to greatness will come long before the arrival of the new heaven and the new earth. The chronology of these events is somewhat complicated, in light of the different interpretations alluded to above, so I will spare you the pain. What I wish to emphasize is the notion of greatness available to the believer. Notice, once again, that believers will have positions of authority, reigning with Christ for a thousand years. Whether or not the thousand years are to be taken literally or figuratively, it is safe to assume that the believer's greatness will be sustained well beyond the thousand years, throughout eternity.

The state of affairs depicted in Revelation is more definitive in the sense that the believers will have come out of a period of severe suffering and trials. Some of them will be martyred because of their testimony for Jesus and because of the word of God. After they die, they will be ushered into glory where the status quo will be changed immediately. Those who took away their lives will be ruled by their victims, the very people they killed. What a contrast! Just when they thought they rid the world of believers, they realize, to their utter shock, that they only succeeded in changing their victims into heavenly royalty of eternal proportions! Hence we see that besides the physical transformation of their bodies from flesh, blood and bones to a point of shining like the sun, believers will be given positions of authority, by Jesus Christ, where they will judge the world and reign with Christ.

The implications of these passages for our lives as believers turn out to be enormous. Whereas we need to pursue our careers and be the best we could ever possibly be in our skills and talents, we need not have regrets over missed opportunities that could have taken us higher. We need not regret, for example, that we lost our bid for elected office, or that we failed our interviews for those well-paying jobs, or that we did not become as rich as we would have liked. In the first place, all these are human achievements which will eventually fade. Scripture reminds us that they are like grass and their glories like the flowers of the field. The grass withers and flowers fall, we are reminded, but the word of the Lord stands forever.[6] Not only will these earthly achievements cease, but those who believe in the Lord Jesus will last forever. Their glory will last forever; for it will be the glory endowed upon them by their Lord Jesus Christ.

Hence Christians need not be side-tracked by the scorn they must endure in the workplace. They need not be intimidated by the postulates of unbelieving scholars in the academia. They need not fear the ridicule thrown at them whenever they take a stand against blatantly immoral behavior (like pre-marital sex and homosexuality) sanctioned by the liberal media. These mild forms of persecution must come. Christ promised the believer to expect them.[7]

What Christians need to be more concerned about is whether they will maintain their stand in the midst of such attempts by the secular world to subjugate them to second-class citizens. If they can only hold their ground to the end, they would be the sorts of believers beheaded "because of their testimony for Jesus Christ" and because of their stand for the word of God. The joy of it all comes in the promise that they will reign with Christ forever and ever.

When I was a student in high school, I was a classroom representative. Such a position came with its own package of privileges. It also came with its share of responsibilities. One such responsibility was to rally the students behind a certain cause. We had been informed that our country's head of state would be touring our school. Hence the district commissioner, in whose jurisdiction the school fell, happened to stop by the school to ensure that all was ready for the president's arrival. Since I was one of those responsible for part of the preparations, someone directed the commissioner to me without my knowing about it.

Before long I was standing face to face with this highly respected district official, talking with him. There was only one problem: I addressed him as if he was one of the high school students in my school. I had no idea that this very person standing before me was a highly ranked government official. What made it worse, the official did nothing whatsoever to declare his status. I simply talked with

---

6   See, for example, Isaiah 40:6 – 8 and I Peter 1:24 – 25.

7   See John 15: 18 – 21

him as I would have talked with my schoolmates. By the time I was done, some students who knew this man's rank in government came over to me with horrified looks on their faces. When they knew they could not be heard they asked me, "Why would you talk to the district commissioner like that?" When the reality of the question finally sank in, a leaf would have knocked me unconscious.

I suspect this is only a very mild reflection of the shock the world will get when it truly discovers who believers really are in God's eyes. In this lifetime believers could be small in the eyes of the world. As some, like Karl Marx, have suggested, they might appear demented to our contemporary society. They could even come across as old-fashioned and closed-minded in this postmodern world. Just the same, what the world considers small, demented, old-fashioned or closed-minded is the very path that God has carved for believers to tread upon on their way to greatness. It is the very path that will finally result in the believer's shining like the sun, reigning with Christ forever and ever. Then is when we will truly experience what it means to be a chosen people, a royal priesthood, and a people belonging to God (1 Peter 2:9). The citizens of heaven will indeed be great.

C. God Will Reveal His Greatness

One of the most difficult things to do in discussing God is the attempt to define His greatness; for God's greatness is infinite by definition. A definition by nature sets limits. So how can one set limits on what is already infinite? The best that I hope to do here, therefore, is to describe a little of what the Bible says about God's greatness in the hope that this will give us a glimpse of just how great the designer of heaven is. Only a great God can design a great city and allow sinners like us to be its great inhabitants.

To be sure, the first thing that will strike us when we cross over to the other side will not be the greatness of heaven's capital city. I believe the first thing that will strike us with such profundity will be the greatness of God. What we shall behold at that time will be a being beyond comprehension, beyond description, and beyond our wildest expectations. Your heart's indescribable spiritual thirst will find consummate satisfaction when it beholds the only being that will fully quench its thirst. Saint Augustine reminded us that our hearts are restless until they find rest in God. On that day, this rest will be fully realized when we behold our Lord face to face.

What kind of being, then, shall we see? What kind of God will our eyes behold? We will see a being of unmatched greatness in beauty, splendor, majesty and glory. Our earthly response to greatness is usually characterized by a wowed feeling, evidenced by jaws dropping with awe. Moreover, once we come to terms with the greatness we behold here on earth, we usually move on to something else, appreciating the instance of greatness we just beheld, but desiring more instances of greatness yet to be seen. I submit, however, that when we behold the greatness of God, we will be eternally wowed by what we will see, and we will not desire to see anything else. Every time we see him (and it seems we shall see him all the time!) we will never cease to say that greatness-capturing word "wow."

I must note, though, that without recourse to Scripture's delineation of greatness, all such talk about God's greatness is at best speculative. Let me therefore take you, the reader, to some passages of Scripture that give us a clue about God's greatness. One that immediately comes to mind is the following passage in Exodus 33:12 – 25. In that passage, Moses almost sounds as if he is demanding God to reveal himself. But God's response is riveting. He is willing to reveal himself to Moses, but insists that his face remains hidden as an act of mercy. The passage reads as follows:

> Moses said to the Lord, "You have been telling me, 'Lead these people,' but you have not let me know whom you will send with me. You have said, 'I know you by name and you have found favor with me.' If you are pleased with me, teach me your ways so I may know you and continue to find favor with you. Remember that this nation is your people." The Lord replied, "My presence will go with you, and I will give you rest." Then Moses said to him, "If your presence does not go with us, do not send us up from here. How will anyone know that you are pleased with me and with your people unless you go with us?

What else will distinguish me and your people from all the other people on the face of the earth?" And the Lord said to Moses, "I will do the very thing you have asked, because I am pleased with you and I know you by name. Then Moses said, "Now show me your glory." And the Lord said, "I will cause all my goodness to pass in front of you, and I will proclaim my name, the Lord, in your presence. I will have mercy on whom I will have mercy, and I will have compassion on whom I will have compassion. But," he said, "you cannot see my face, for no one may see me and live."

This passage reveals an interesting thing about God. His greatness is such that *human beings cannot behold his face without subjecting themselves to obliteration.* Flesh, blood and bones are all we are made of, and we are ill-equipped, in our cognitive faculties, to contain the presence of God should he choose to reveal himself in his fullest majesty.

It is therefore no wonder, for example, that when Isaiah had the chance to behold the throne of God, he was immediately aware of how dangerously close to death he was in the presence of such divine holiness. Even more spellbinding is the fact that when Peter, James and John beheld Jesus at the Mount of Transfiguration, they fell down in fear and trembling, unable to contain the splendor of their Lord and Savior. Notice that every time we get even the slightest glimpse of God's revelation, we are immediately overcome by a feeling of fear or dread, of which C. S. Lewis talks about in the first chapter of his book, *The Problem of Pain.* That is why whenever angels revealed themselves to God's people, whether in the Old or in the New Testament, the angels had to address their fear by urging them not to be afraid of the unusual appearance they countenanced. This underscores the fact that when we see the greatness of something beyond this world, we cower in fear. How much more shall our sinful nature be overwhelmed, indeed fatally overrun, by God's full majesty, should he choose to fully reveal himself!

This goes to show that seeing God face to face cannot be compared with seeing an earthly celebrity. It cannot be compared to physically attending a presidential inauguration. It cannot be compared to shaking the hands of your favorite sports icon. Neither can it be compared to meeting a famous author and getting an autographed copy of his best-selling volume. Celebrities, presidents, sports icons and all those in their caliber are mere human beings with human weaknesses just like the rest of us. Oddly enough, we have deified them. We feel that they have achieved an aura of greatness in light of their accomplishments in life. But we know, deep down in our hearts, that celebrities make mistakes. Many make bad decisions. Some commit crimes. Others get caught up in scandals. As this book goes to print, accusations of scandals upon scandals are mounting on respected public figures and celebrities.

With God, however, things are different. If we ever get the chance to see him, we will be looking at a being who makes no mistakes. We will find ourselves before a being too holy to behold sin, a being with no weaknesses, a being immune from scandals, and one who, without question, commands the attention of everything he has created. We will be looking at Ultimate Perfection, whose cognition penetrates the very core of our being, with complete knowledge of our most intimate thoughts, secrets and desires. On the day his Son comes for us, we will see why he is properly the Celebrity of Celebrities.

It would seem that the only reason we will be able to see God and live is because in heaven we will have glorified bodies, bodies transformed in a way that, at the sight of God, will be attracted to him. While still here on earth, though, our bodies are completely unable to contain the full revelation of God's divine majesty and glory. To be sure, God's withholding of his self-disclosure to us here on earth is in itself an act of mercy. He knows we cannot handle his full glory if he revealed himself in the fullness of his splendor.

This idea is somewhat illustrated, in a woefully inadequate way, by an incident I witnessed as a student in high school. I was in a physics class conducting some laboratory experiments with my classmates. One of the students in the class absent-mindedly plugged a flashlight bulb into a two-hundred and forty volt electric outlet. Immediately he flipped the switch on, a frightening bang followed.

After ensuring that he was not hurt in the incident, we curiously examined what was left of the bulb. It was completely obliterated.

By analogy, if God were to reveal his full glory to all humanity in this lifetime, we will be infinitely worse than that electric bulb; for we will be plugging our limited human capacities into an outlet of Omnipotence. This does not involve merely plugging human power into a two-hundred and forty volt power outlet. It involves much more. It involves plugging human power into Infinite Power. Our sinful flesh and blood simply cannot handle God's full revelation of himself. Those who demand that God should reveal himself in his full majesty, quite frankly, have no idea of what they are asking God to do. Hence, they have no idea of the potential danger of such a request, should God choose to honor it. It is indeed an act of mercy that God chooses not to reveal his fullness to us; rather he has mercifully revealed himself in the humility of the person of Christ.

However, once our bodies are glorified, we will have the privilege of seeing God's great majesty, and the benefit of living eternally in that majestic glory. We will at once realize that he is infinitely greater than any king we have ever known. We will see how it is that he is infinitely more powerful than all the empires of the world's history put together. We will see how it was that his power held all the elements of the universe together. We know that earthly rulers depend on nature to conduct their business. By a much higher token, we will see how nature depends on God to conduct its business. He will be above all rule, dominion and power.

I submit that we will see, on that day, how it was that we lived in him and moved in him and had our being in him right here on earth. We will somehow understand how, in his great plan, things that could have gone wrong did not go wrong and how he often snatched us from the hands of the enemy. We will see how in his great wisdom he weaved the many events in our lives, not only to accomplish his purposes, but also to benefit us spiritually.

Thus once we come face to face with God's greatness, we will at once bow down and worship him. It will be spontaneous, yet uncoerced. It will be a natural response to the unparalleled glory that we will find ourselves beholding. Our ascriptions of glory to

Him will strike us as woefully inadequate to the extent that we will feel pleasantly indebted to do it again and again.

Maxie Dunnam, president emeritus of Asbury Theological Seminary always reminded us never to tell God how great our mountains are. Rather, he urged, we should tell our mountains how great our God is. By that claim he seemed to urge believers not to spend time focusing on the greatness of their problems and forgetting about the greatness of God. God's greatness is far above the challenges presented by our daily lives. Without diminishing the seriousness of such challenges, we are still urged to keep our focus on God's greatness, for ultimately, that is what we will see at the end of our journey.

The hope of seeing God's greatness is surely a healing balm to the tired and weary saint, overcome by pain, sorrow and suffering. The greatness of God assures *that* believer that our troubles will soon be over. Moreover, it gives the believer the desire to live through life's difficult days in the hope that better days are coming. In light of these, the weary believer can still find strength to speak to the mountains of life about the greatness of the One who will return to redeem the suffering saint.

Heaven therefore is a place of greatness. It will have a great city, which will be inhabited by great citizens. It will also be ruled by our Great and Almighty God. It is a hope that can be found nowhere else. When you think about it, hope in this world can only be available from the person who created this world. It cannot be found in some other different source. This is not all we find about heaven. There is more.

III. Heaven is a Place of Eternal Beauty

We have seen from the previous chapter that greatness will be a major theme in heaven. Another theme commonly associated with heaven is the theme of beauty. In my first year of high school, my religious education teacher asked us to pretend we were selling a commodity (in this case it was a shirt) and to design a poster that advertized that commodity. I simply started writing about the shirt, extolling its virtues with the most eloquent words I could muster at that time. My poster consisted of about 100 words of mere rhetoric.

However, the fellow sitting next to me decided to use a different method. He began by drawing a picture of a shirt, and used colors to make it as beautiful and as attractive as he could. By the time he was done, the shirt had all sorts of colors on it, with just a few phrases here and there describing its features, like "easily buttoned," "wrinkle free," "two side pockets," and so on. When we submitted our posters, mine was rejected. It was too wordy for the teacher's taste. My friend's poster was immediately accepted, and was used as an example for the rest of the class to emulate. The reason was simple: it was beautiful and attractive. Very few words were needed to market it. "Its simple beauty was worth a thousand words," we were promptly reminded.

This serves to underscore an important aspect about human beings. No matter where we look, it seems that humans everywhere have a desire for beauty. We seek enthrallment from things we consider aesthetically appealing. A young man, for example, wishes

29

to get married to a woman he thinks is beautiful. Film-making companies assign leading roles to individuals considered good looking by the society. We are always attracted to beautiful music. We stop to admire beautiful sunsets and the starry skies at night. We desire to live in beautiful houses. Most of us wish we owned beautiful cars. Beauty sells as easily as it attracts.

By contrast, we shy away from what, in our opinion, strikes us as ugly and undesirable. The story of a mother who rescued her daughter from a burning house powerfully illustrates this. The mother is said to have been out of the house in which her daughter was sleeping. She had run out of salt, and thus stopped by her neighbor's house to get some for her midday cooking. On her way back, she saw, to her dismay, that her house was on fire. Her first and immediate concern was for her daughter who was sleeping inside. She rushed to the scene, crashed through the door, and ran into her daughter's bedroom and found her daughter overwhelmed with smoke, choking and crying. She picked her up quickly, ran out of the fiercely burning house, with the roof caving in immediately after. In the process of saving her daughter, she got severely burned, burns that scarred her entire body. The scars remained with her for the rest of her life.

As her daughter matured into her teenage years, she was somewhat embarrassed by the scars she saw all over her mother's face and hands. She hated it when her mother came to pick her up from school. She neither desired nor took the time to know the cause of her mother's scars. One morning, feeling overwhelmed with embarrassment and shame at being seen with a parent that looked neither presentable nor attractive, she decided to ask her mother about those scars. When her mother finally told her the story, the teenage daughter could no longer hold back her tears. Suddenly, her mother's scars, previously ugly to the daughter, became marks of such great beauty and pride.

This underscores the fact that we all seem to desire the beautiful and shy away, perhaps even despise, what we think is ugly. No one wants to associate with what one thinks or believes is ugly. The ugly, in our opinion, is bad, hence undesirable. By contrast, however, everyone seems to desire the beautiful; for we believe that what is beautiful is good and glorious. We are convinced, beyond a shadow of doubt that beauty attracts. Expressing our desire for beauty and dislike for the ugly is exactly how God designed us, and because of this, he ensures that our final destination will somehow address this need, giving us a glimpse of Ultimate Beauty. Our look at Scripture, then, allows us to make some observations about the beauty of heaven.

A. The Beauty of Heaven's City

The book of Revelation talks of a beautiful city called the New Jerusalem. Beginning with a description of the beauty of its walls, we read the following words:

> The wall was made of jasper, and the city of pure gold, as pure as glass. The foundations of the city walls were decorated with every kind of precious stone. The first foundation was jasper, the second sapphire, the third chalcedony, the fourth emerald, the fifth sardonyx, the sixth carnelian, the seventh chrysolite, the eighth, beryl, the ninth topaz, the tenth chrysoprase, the eleventh jacinth, and the twelfth amethyst. The twelve gates were twelve pearls, each gate made of a single pearl. The great street of the city was of pure gold, like transparent glass.[8]

I well recall the first time I set my eyes on the capital city of my home country. I could not believe the endless beauty of the lights and their different colors as they began to light the city at dusk. They seemed so pure and aesthetically attractive. On one of the nights I got onto an elevator of one of the tallest buildings in the city and rode it up to the top floor. I wanted to get the best possible view of the city that I could find. When I finally got to the top floor, I looked out through the window at the seemingly endless sea of different colors of lights. The experience was amazing, given that I had come from the rural countryside, and could then see that which I, previously, only read about in geography textbooks.

---

8   Revelation 21:18 – 21

What took me by surprise, however, was the reality that lay underneath those lights. Despite the purity, brightness and beauty of the lights, the city turned out to be quite filthy in many aspects. During the day one could not help being disgusted with mounds of garbage that littered different blocks and streets. The roughness of the city dwellers was revolting at times. The street children contributed to the nightmare. I was always left wondering why no one did anything to sort out the mess. Sometimes I wondered whether the government was indifferent to the plight of those street children, who not only lived on handouts they received from sympathetic citizens, but also demanded for them sometimes, as if they had a right to those handouts. Thankfully, for some of them, non-profit making organizations came to their rescue in different ways.

When I later accepted a job as a pastor in one of the churches in that city, I was informed that one of my pastoral jobs involved home to home visitation, which happened mostly in the evenings. One such evening, very close to the midnight hour, I was on my way home, on foot, from a pastoral visitation. I could not believe my eyes when I saw a group of young men pounce on an innocent passerby, taking all of his belongings with them. Of course I could not help him. I was no match for the group of young men. It was such a large group that all of them could have easily overpowered me.

Many months later I witnessed another instance of mugging before my very eyes. I had just traveled overnight from my rural home town, and was reporting for duty at my city church. As I sat in the bus waiting for it to take off, a smartly dressed man was attacked by a group of about five strong men, who twisted his arm, lifted him up in the air and took off his shoes, then dropped him and quickly disappeared with his briefcase. I could only guess what the valuables contained in that case might have been as the victim staggered in disbelief, trying to make sense of what had just happened to him.

Perhaps the most heart-rending experience was when I alighted from a bus one morning and waited for my next bus. As I waited by that terminal, out of nowhere and without warning, four men jumped in front of a small Daihatsu Charade that was approaching an intersection right before me. They quickly pulled off their guns, trained it on the Asian driver, forced him out of the car and then bundled him into the car's backseat. One of the car-jackers took the wheel and sped off at top speed with their victim. I could only imagine what might have happened to the poor Asian driver. Days apart from that incident, I saw the lifeless body of a newborn baby hanging by a string, which was itself laced around a barbed wire fence. Evidently, a homeless street mother had given birth to this child. Just how the child ended up on that noose defies imagination. For a long time I could not believe the different instances of pain I was witnessing in the city almost on a weekly basis.

I gradually came to discover that the beauty of the city lights that I had grown to appreciate was really a camouflage of what was happening on the ground. For many months I longed for a restoration of the beauty of that city. Unfortunately, the public seemed to have lost confidence in the city's administration, beginning with the mayor himself all the way down to the city clerk. They did not think these individuals were capable of doing much. The city's infrastructure was quickly failing. The more I thought about these, the more I got concerned that perhaps the beauty of the city would never be restored in my lifetime if at all.

By contrast, consider the beauty of the precious stones mentioned in the passage above. For one, their exact nature is unclear. Nevertheless, the Bible seems to present them as objects of incomparable beauty. There seems to be no earthly examples with which we could compare some of the stones. So far no earthly eye has seen or even comprehended the nature of their beauty. Perhaps that is why we are unable to determine their exact nature.

Compare their beauty with the cities we live in. Our houses are made of bricks, which, in only a matter of years begin to fall apart. A number of them need serious repair. Many of them will be demolished within the next few decades. Think about the streets of those cities. Most of them get littered with garbage, cigarette butts, empty beer cans, empty soda cans, plastic paper bags, bird droppings, oil-dripping cars, and filthy sidewalks.

However, the promise we get about our city in heaven, including the home our Lord has gone to prepare for us, is nothing short of spectacular. Your home in heaven comes with a different story. It comes in a neat incomparable and unbeatable package. Think about it. There will be no abandoned houses, no condemned houses, no trashcans, no garbage, no garbage trucks and no sewage systems. I doubt that we will ever need them. Our city and home in heaven will, on the one hand, lack everything believers hate to see in a city. On the other hand it will have everything they have ever wanted to see in a city.

The streets will be clean. The houses will be breathtaking. The landscape will be spellbinding. The grounds will be stunning. The sounds will be amazing. The scenery will be flabbergasting. The people will be trustworthy. Its government will be impeccable, impeachable, unbeatable, incomparable, and infallible. It will have excellent delivery of services. It will have "timely" execution of responsibilities. It will have unrivaled beauty, astonishing structure, and off-the-charts perfection. That will be your house and home in heaven.

Hence, whereas it is good to be concerned about the poor structure of the houses that some of us live in, we do not need to worry about the longevity of their ugliness, for it is only a matter of time before such ugliness is gone. Neither should such ugliness be an indicator of our status before God. This is an attitude we should adopt as believers, irrespective of whether we live in an apartment, a studio, a rented house, a duplex, a housing project or in the streets. Of course this does not mean that we should do nothing about the undesirable living conditions in which we might find ourselves. Living well and comfortably is something we should try to achieve as much as possible. However, the fact that we cannot attain desirable living conditions does not in any way lower our social status before God. Irrespective of where we live, our standing before God is clear. We are citizens of heaven, and Christ is preparing a place for us. God is preparing a beautiful city, indeed, a beautiful mansion for us in a home beyond this physical universe.

B. The Beauty of Heaven's Citizens

Having considered the beauty of the city, we now turn to the beauty of the citizens of heaven. Human beings desire the beautiful, and only God can fulfill the heart's longing for true beauty. Indeed, as the lyrics of the famous worship song remind us, only God can make all things beautiful, including human beings, at a time of his own choosing.

Consider the many ways in which our desire for personal beauty is expressed. The cosmetic industries try to lure us into buying their products so we could look better. The weight-loss industries lure us into buying their products by appealing, sometimes falsely, to our desire to lose more weight. The plastic surgeons fill us with the hope of reversing our graying hair or replenishing our receding hairlines. It would be an understatement to suggest that, collectively, we have spent millions of dollars trying to achieve that ideal beauty.

It has been said that beauty is in the eyes of the beholder. A possible implication of this claim is that what one person considers beautiful, in many cases, is not what another person would consider beautiful. More accurately, the claim goes, we all possess within ourselves different standards for beauty. The claimants thus conclude that our judgments about beauty are quite subjective. For example, most of those living in the southern parts of the United States believe that a sunny day is a beautiful one. While some of those in the north believe that a snowy, wintry day is more beautiful.

Of course there is some truth to the claim that our beauty judgments are subjective. Nevertheless, this is not true of all of life. I believe that the biblical depiction of beauty as portrayed in heaven points to Ultimate Beauty. By this I refer to the sort of beauty to which all citizens of heaven will acquiesce. When they finally see this Beauty, they will all concur with one voice that it is indeed beautiful.

However, while still on this earth, we must admit that the reality of suffering deals a severe blow to the notion of beauty. In my first year in Bible School, a friend of mine was severely burned when a cooking gas cylinder exploded in his house. He had burns all over his body, which scalded his skin, drastically changing his appearance in a way that could only be described as horrific. Even though he recovered completely from the burns, his skin was never fully restored. His hands, legs and face were filled with scars that painfully reminded him of that fateful day. In spite of this, my friend Hudson never lost his joy. He always looked forward to the day he believed the Lord Jesus would restore him completely. He never ceased to tell me that the Lord was still doing plastic surgery on his body. Several years after graduating from Bible College Hudson died unexpectedly in a tragic car wreck.

Hudson lived his life as fully as he could, inspired by the hope of the beauty of heaven, the restoration of his body, and a final reunion with God in that promised eternal relationship with him. His hope of heaven gives us an aspect of its beauty that will be depicted by those who will inhabit it. We get a glimpse of this from the following passage, which I quoted in the previous chapter: "Dear friends, now we are children of God, and what we will be has not yet been made known. But we know that when he appears, we shall be like him, for we shall see him as he is. Everyone who has this hope in him purifies himself, just as he is pure."[9] The Bible here is not exactly clear about the beauty that God will bestow on our physical features, but the hope that such beauty will be unsurpassable is hard to miss.

Consider first the claim, alluded to earlier, that the saints of God will shine like the stars. A late night walk in rural Africa can reveal the grandeur of the starry heavens on a cloudless sky. The beauty captured by the numberless stars in the sky is simply breathtaking. Seeing such beauty as a young child led me to believe I was beholding a city hanging upside down! Only a night in a rural village in Africa, or in some third world country away from a modern city, can reveal such beauty. Not even this kind of beauty, or something analogous to it, comes close to what God promises to bestow upon his saints in glory.

A more elaborate passage captures the beauty of heaven's citizens in the following way: "But our citizenship is in heaven. And we eagerly await a savior from there, the Lord Jesus Christ, who, by the power that enables him to bring everything under his control,

---

9   I John 3:2

will transform our lowly bodies so that they will be like his glorious body."[10] According to this passage, our bodies will be transformed into what theologians have called "glorified bodies."

What kinds of bodies will these be? Notice the contrast between "lowly" and "glorified." It would seem to be the case here that lowly bodies are weak and subject to corruption, decay and death. By contrast, glorified bodies are far superior to the current bodies that human beings have. Such bodies will not be corrupted. They will not suffer decay. Neither will they succumb to death. Moreover, such bodies will no longer be overcome by the power of sin; for the power of sin will not only be defeated; sin itself will also be eliminated.

The Apostle Paul makes this clear in the following words: "So will it be with the resurrection of the dead. The body that is sown is perishable, it is raised imperishable; it is sown in dishonor, it is raised in glory; it is sown in weakness, it is raised in power; it is sown a natural body, it is raised a spiritual body."[11]

What we see here is a depiction of the beauty that our resurrected bodies will have. A key term that captures this beauty is "glory." When we consider the meaning of this word in the original language, it gives us fascinating insights about the sort of beauty that will attend the resurrected body. It will be such that those who behold it will give it a respectable opinion as well as honorable consideration. In other words, no longer will you look at yourself in the mirror and wish you looked different. Similarly, no longer will people look at you and suggest things you could do to improve your looks. God will have completed his work of making you beautiful at the resurrection event. You will have a body full of dignity and majesty. Another way of describing it is to think of it as a body endowed with divine ornament, divine pomp, divine magnificence and divine radiance. It will have the kind of luster that can only be described as dazzling. We cannot even think of a way to improve the sort of beautification that the saints of God will undergo once they are glorified.

Thus whereas it is important to do what we can to maintain the overall health of our bodies, we need not lose our heads over

---

10   Philippians 3:20, 21.
11   I Corinthians 15:42 – 44

the sufferings and pains that seem to attack those very bodies. Admittedly, it is a tragic thing that a person can be committed to a wheel chair for the rest of his or her life, by something like a car wreck, when the same individual lived a relatively healthy life on the whole.

Philosopher Roland Puccetti struggles with this very idea when he cites the following example. He asks us to consider a brilliant pianist with a promising career ahead of him. Unfortunately for the pianist, he contracts a disease, Huntington's chorea, at age 35. He then begins to regress physically and psychically, with 15 years, at most, to live. He is then confined to a mental institution, crippled and unable to care for himself.[12] According to Puccetti, if God is merciful, he should either take the pianist's disease away at once, or take away his life instead of prolonging his life for 15 years.[13]

Puccetti is not a believer in God, and refuses to believe in God for reasons such as those provided by the example cited above. For that reason, Puccetti really has no hope of the afterlife. Neither does he have any hope that everything wrong will be made right, whether here on earth or in heaven. Of course the Christian situation is different. The hope of having our bodies beautifully restored in heaven makes our painful experiences endurable here on earth.

That said, a word of caution is necessary. If I stop my explication of the beauty of the saints at this point, I run into a situation similar to Lucifer's. For one, biblical tradition has it that Lucifer was so overcome by his own beauty that pride overtook him and made him desire to rebel against God. Similarly, if we merely stop at the beauty of the saints, not only will we be missing the ultimate goal of heaven – namely, the eternal enjoyment of our relationship with and knowledge of God – we will also be aiming at heaven for selfish reasons. Our intention to get there will be motivated by the desire to be beautiful, and that's it. However, being consumed by our final eternal beauty, without thinking of the ultimate goal of heaven, will

---

12   Roland Puccetti, "The Loving God: Some Observations on Hick's Theodicy," *The Problem of Evil: Selected Readings*, Michael L. Peterson, ed. (Notre Dame: University of Notre Dame Press, 1992), p. 233.

13   Puccetti, p. 239

result in the sin of pride long before we get to heaven – the very sin that got the devil expelled from there. Thus whereas we have been promised eternal beauty, we must remember that such beauty is really peripheral. What is central is that as beautiful as we will all be, our knowledge of God will be finally secured, our relationship with God will be finally restored, and we will be united with God in that state of eternal happiness with him. Quite frankly, nothing will be more beautiful than being reunited with God, the Ultimate Beauty that our souls seek. It is only fitting, therefore, to turn our attention to the beauty of God.

C. The Beauty of God

In a sermon illustrations book entitled *Illustrations for Biblical Preaching*, Michael P. Green cites an interesting description of God's glory. It begins by noting that when we describe the glory of God, we really describe the sum effect of all of his attributes. The glory of God, Green says, is really his grace, his truth, his goodness, his mercy, his justice, his knowledge, his power, his eternality, and all the attributes that God must have in order to be God. For this reason, the Glory of God is intrinsic. In other words, it is essential to God in much the same way that light is essential to the sun, as blue is essential to the sky, and wetness is essential to water. We do not give the sun its light; the sun is light. We do not make the sky blue; it is blue. We do not make water wet; it is wet. Hence in all of these instances, each object has an attribute essential to it.[14]

However, Green observes that with human beings the case is different. Human glory is not intrinsic to humans. They receive their glory from an external source. For example, if you take a king, put away all his robes and crowns, and replace those robes with a rag, and if you take a beggar and place him next to the king, no one will notice the difference. This is because the king has no glory intrinsic to him. The only glory a king will have is the one his fellow subjects will give to him – when his subjects agree to robe him and

---

14   Michael P. Green, ed., *Illustrations for Biblical Preaching* (Grand Rapids: Baker Book House, 1997) p. 167.

place a crown on his head. Hence, the point is that the only glory that human beings have is the one granted to them. However, God's glory is his essentially. It is impossible to take God's glory away from him because glory is his nature. Neither can we add anything to the glory that God already has; for it is his being.[15]

Generally speaking,[16] Green is essentially correct in this regard. Moreover, what is true of God's glory is also true of his beauty. This is because God's glory is really his beauty. What we say of God's glory must also be said of God's beauty. Thus, as with God's glory, we note that when we describe the beauty of God, we really describe the sum effect of all of his attributes. We can say with accuracy, for example, that God's grace, truth, goodness, mercy, justice, knowledge, power and eternality are all beautiful. For this reason, the beauty of God is intrinsic to God. Whereas traditional theology does not quite focus more on the beauty of God, few classical theologians will doubt that God gives us the standard of beauty in much the same way, for example, that he gives us the standard of right and wrong. It would therefore be fair to say that if God is the absolute standard of all values, he must be the absolute standard of all beauty. In fact, it would be fair to add that he is the Absolutely Beautiful Divine Being.

By describing God as a being full of glory, various passages of Scripture point us to the beauty of God, and for that matter, of Jesus Christ. For example, in the account depicting the event on the Mount of Transfiguration, we read the following words:

> After six days, Jesus took Peter, James and John with him and led them up a high mountain, where they were all alone. There he was transfigured before them. His clothes became dazzling white, whiter than anyone in the world could bleach them. And there appeared before them Elijah and Moses, who were talking to Jesus.

---

15 Ibid.

16 I use "generally speaking" here for a simple reason. If taken in some technical sense, it is not the case, for example, that the sky is always blue. It appears blue from our vantage point. At night, however, it seems quite dark. Hence Green's illustration must be taken in layman's terms.

Peter said to Jesus, "Rabbi, it is good for us to be here. Let us put up three shelters – one for you, one for Moses and one for Elijah. (He did not know what to say, they were so frightened). Then a cloud appeared and enveloped them, and a voice came from the cloud: "This is my Son, whom I love. Listen to him!"[17]

Take note of the Bible's description of the divine environment that enveloped Jesus, Peter, James and John. We learn that the clothes of Christ became dazzling white, whiter than any person in the world could bleach them. The original text suggests that no launderer could clean the clothes and bring them anywhere close to the brightness they possessed at that very hour. Presumably, this cleanliness was brought about by the divine environment that presented itself to the beholders. It gives us a pointer to the glory and beauty of God. As Michael Green postulates, it is the kind of glory intrinsic to the one possessing it, namely, God. It is not the kind of glory that could be given to God, even though we do worship God as if to glorify him. His true glory is such that no one could bestow it on him.

It is this very glory that shines through the city of the New Jerusalem. Several times the Bible depicts it as follows:

> And he carried me away in the Spirit to a mountain great and high, and showed me the Holy City, Jerusalem, coming down out of heaven from God. It shone with the glory of God, and its brilliance was like that of a very precious jewel, like a jasper, clear as crystal.[18]

Of this city we read again the following words: "The city does not need the sun or the moon to shine on it, for the glory of God gives it light, and the Lamb is its lamp. The nations will walk by its light and the kings of the earth will bring their splendor into it."[19]

The glory of God and the beauty of God go hand in hand. To use a very earthly expression, they are "both sides of the same coin."

---

17 Mark 9:2 – 8
18 Revelation 21:10 – 11
19 Revelation 21: 23, 24.

We learn that this beauty, depicted by his glory, will light up the city. When believers will at last set their eyes on the glory and majesty of God, it will be the most beautiful sight they will ever see. Believers will never fully understand beauty until they see it in its absolute nature; for when they see it, everything else that they considered beautiful will pale in comparison to the sight that will present itself to their glorified eyes. Once they behold that Absolutely Beautiful sight, they will be fully convinced that nothing else, and no one else, could be more beautiful. Moreover, since what is beautiful is always attractive, they will at once be eternally attracted to the Beauty and Glory of God in a way that satisfies their deepest longings and desires – the longing and desire to always be one with that which attracts them, with that which they find themselves willingly loving.

An example from our everyday experience should help to clarify this. Beauty attracts. As noted earlier, movie directors always look for good-looking actors (by their standards, of course) to assume leading roles in their movies. Every year *People* magazine features articles depicting the best-looking[20] individual of the year. Somehow we believe, rightly or wrongly, that the good is frequently associated with the beautiful. We are attracted by beautiful lights, beautiful clothes, beautiful houses, beautiful cars and beautiful people. We always long for the beautiful. Indeed, we always have the desire to be one with what we consider beautiful. Once we have it in our possession, we feel a sense of delight (though in many cases the delight is temporary). For this reason, when we see what we believe is beautiful, we do our best to get it, especially if we believe we can get it – whatever it is.

At my wedding day, seeing my bride-to-be at the end of the aisle, waiting to come to the altar, was an experience beyond description. She was more beautiful than I first thought. To think that she was coming to the altar to be united to me in Holy Matrimony just sent a jolt of electricity inside me. By the time she reached the altar, my heart was racing wildly. I knew that I was being joined, not only by the vows I would make before everyone present, but also by God himself. When we both finally said, "I do," the feeling of "having

---

20 To be sure, *People* magazine normally uses a more graphic expression.

arrived" overwhelmed me. I had waited thirty six years for this day, and it had finally come.

Let us now take this notion to the eternal realm. The book of Revelation uses the analogy of a "bride-and-groom relationship" to capture the nature of our relationship with Christ. The return of Christ, for example, is referred to as the wedding supper of the Lamb, and the church is the bride, dressed in fine linen bright and clean (see Revelation 19:7-8).

As noted above, one of the first things that will strike us with great profundity when we set our glorified eyes on God will be his Divine Beauty: He will present himself to us as Absolute Beauty. His beauty will be such that once we see it, we will understand why no human mind could have possibly figured it out, imagined it, or creatively invented it. As noted above, once we see that Absolutely Beautiful sight of the Eternal Triune God, we will at once be attracted to him. His sight will be infinitely delightful to behold. He will appear to us as Beauty in the most attractive and purest form. As soon as we see him, we will have the divine urge to be united with him in an eternal relationship of love, joy and happiness.

Even more amazing is the following realization: we will be embarrassed to discover that this Absolute Beauty is what we were running away from when we rebelled against him here on earth. *How could we be so depraved as to turn away from someone as Beautiful as our Triune God!* This will be an expression of many a saint. Within this context, it would be fair to say that once we see that Divine Beauty, we will find our love for him irresistible. Moreover, our love for him will be such a delight that we shall never grow tired of it.

Heaven is therefore a place of eternal beauty. Its capital city will be beautiful; its citizens will be beautiful; and once the citizens come face to face with God in their glorified bodies, they will at once discover how Absolutely Beautiful God truly is. God has in store for his children a wonderful place of great delight and joy. It is a place that no person should miss – a deal that no thinking person should turn down.

IV. Heaven Is A Place of Eternal Healing

Heaven is therefore both a place of greatness and a place of eternal beauty. We now turn to the motif of healing that heaven will present to us. There is no doubt that we live in a broken world in desperate need of healing. As I write this chapter, a devastating earthquake has brought both the nation of Chile and the Island of Haiti to their knees. Images of rescue workers and injured citizens of Haiti have been flashing across living room television screens across the globe for weeks. Chile is of no exception. Questions have been asked as to why a good God would allow this to happen. Various answers have been given, ranging from blaming all Haitians for making a pact with the devil (an explanation I flatly reject) to, quite erroneously, calling God's existence to question.

Besides the Chilean and Haitian earthquakes, the dust has not yet settled from the devastating effects of the earthquake in China, from the aftereffects of Hurricane Katrina and from the shocking aftermath of the Indonesian tsunami. Hundreds of thousands of people died in all these catastrophes. All these have pushed other instances of equally intense suffering to the periphery. I speak here of the starving citizens of certain drought-stricken countries in Africa, the crisis in Darfur region of the Sudan, and inter-ethnic violence in Kenya, Rwanda and Democratic Republic of the Congo.

Besides these different incidents of tragedy on a wide scale, we are also, on a relatively narrower scale, painfully aware of the instances of suffering crippling those we love. We will all have to go through suffering of some kind at some stage in our lives. We seem to be aware of at least one person close to us whose life has been stricken with indescribable pain.

I remember for example, Sister Betty Davis[21] – one of the most beautiful persons my wife and I ever met at Duncan Chapel, Jimtown United Methodist Church. Sister Betty was a saint, if I ever saw one. Her humor was contagious. She is fondly remembered as a person who had so many friends in her lifetime that it was difficult to imagine a friendlier person existed. It was said that Sister Betty could, with perfect ease, hold three conversations simultaneously – one on her cell phone, another on her regular phone, and the third with a visiting friend at her house. She brought a lot of joy to her family. Everything seemed to be going well with Betty. She was an active member of the church, evidenced by her willingness to hold the position of church treasurer. She was also a devoted member of the church choir. On several occasions members of the church choir held their choir rehearsals at her house.

One Sunday morning, my wife and I drove to church, parked the car, and walked into the fellowship hall of the church through the kitchen door. Sister Betty was standing in the kitchen wearing her usual good-to-see-you smile. We hugged her good morning and, absentmindedly asked her how she was doing. She took the question seriously, and as I hugged another member of the church, Betty said, "I've got cancer."

I knew that was what she said, but I turned around to her in a state of obvious denial and disbelief. "What? You've got cancer?" I asked. "What type of cancer?" She then told us how she visited the doctor and was diagnosed with breast cancer. Somehow I had an inner sense of cautious relief, convincing myself that breast cancer, if detected early enough, is not necessarily a death sentence. Just the same, I was still horrified by the news; for previously, the church had just buried Mary Warfield, another cancer victim.

---

21 I use this story with permission from James Davis, Betty's surviving husband.

Betty started her rounds of chemotherapy, which wore her out. Somehow we were assured she would make it. We desperately prayed for her healing. For some time it seemed as if her cancer was in remission. As days and months went by, it was becoming clear to us that Sister Betty was not doing too well. One morning, while on a speaking engagement in Dallas, Texas, my wife called me, telling me that Betty's cancer had spread to her lungs. "It is only a matter of time," she said.

This was devastating news. After my speaking engagement, I flew back to Lexington, Kentucky, and had the chance to visit with Sister Betty. She seemed to be aware that she was about to pass on to glory. She assured us that she knew of her position in the Lord Jesus Christ. She seemed to know that even though the cancer was eating her life away, her healing on the other side was a guarantee.

Betty passed on to glory on the Holy Week of April 2006 and was buried the following Monday, after Easter Sunday. Her funeral was a mixture of sweetness and sorrow. She had lived her life well, and we celebrated that. Nevertheless, her family, and those who knew her, felt and expressed excruciating pain at her departure. It was difficult for me to put together the kind of eulogy that expressed the joy of her relationship with Christ while, at the same time, be mindful of the pain she went through. It was equally difficult for my wife and me to watch James Davis and his daughters lay their loved one to rest. We watched them suffer and felt their pain.

However, one word of hope and assurance kept ringing in my mind. I felt that having crossed over to glory, Sister Betty was ready for her healing. The assurance of her healing would come as promised in the following words from Revelation 21:3-4:

> And I heard a loud voice from the throne saying, "Now the dwelling of God is with men, and he will live with them. They will be his people, and God himself will be with them and be their God. He will wipe every tear from their eyes. There will be no more death or mourning or crying or pain, for the old order of things has passed away."

The passage underscores the hope of healing that will be fulfilled for all believers. It is a hope of healing from physical and emotional pain. Allow me to say that this is a hope unavailable in other systems of thought. The hope of restoration and healing, it would seem to me, is available only in the promise given to us by Jesus Christ. That is why I wish to explore the different types of healing God's word promises us as we live through this broken world.

A. Healing From Physical Suffering

The promise for healing from physical suffering includes healing from suffering brought about by natural processes of the sort mentioned at the introduction of this chapter. To see the nature of this promise, consider these words from Revelation 22:1-3:

> Then the angel showed me the river of the water of life, as clear as crystal, flowing from the throne of God and of the Lamb, down the middle of the great street of the city. On each side of the river stood the tree of life, bearing twelve crops of fruit, yielding its fruit every month. And the leaves of the tree are for the healing of the nations. No longer will there be any curse. The throne of God and of the Lamb will be in the city, and his servants will serve him.

The world was first cursed when God pronounced judgment on the serpent, on Eve and on Adam. This very curse is now taken away in the book of Revelation. I contend here that the claim "No longer will there be any curse" refers to the curse brought about by the sin of Adam and Eve. It is not limited, though, to just that curse alone, for the nature of the language suggests, in fact, that all curses will be done away with completely. However, the curse in Genesis, I hold, is what seems to be responsible for the brokenness of our world, for it came about as a consequence of the sin of our first ancestors.

Hence, the curse is reversed, healing is pronounced, and physical suffering is removed from our midst. Nature is restored to what God originally intended it to be – a perfect working order of his divine creation. The river of the water of life as well as the tree of life standing on each side of the river both assure us of the physical healing of the processes of nature.

At the very least, what the Bible seems to underscore in the text above is a future realization of a world without earthquakes, tornadoes, hurricanes, tsunamis, destructive thunderstorms and illnesses of all kinds. We are assured that these will not affect God's children anymore. A world without such catastrophes will not only be beautiful, as the previous chapter has already argued; it will also be a healed world. I intend to give this view a separate treatment in the third section on this chapter.

For now, however, allow me to note that a healed earth, analogous to this healed world, is envisioned in 2 Chronicles 7:14. After King Solomon dedicated the temple to God and offered numerous sacrifices, God responded to Solomon's prayer in the following way: "If my people, who are called by my name, will humble themselves and pray and seek my face and turn from their wicked ways, then will I hear from heaven and forgive their sin and heal their land."

The promise is given to the children of Israel in a way that seems to anticipate a future state of rebellion that will somewhat bring about, as a consequence, natural disasters and physical suffering. God's view seems to be that these natural calamities will be reversed when some kind of character reformation takes place in the lives of his children, namely, humility, prayer, worship and repentance.

We also have the promise of healing from sufferings of a more personal and intimate nature, like those sufferings brought about by illnesses. They are personal and intimate in that they are internal to the person with the illness in question. Once again, in the previous chapter, we noted that the ugliness and deformities brought about by these illnesses will be done away with. If we paused there, however, we will only be telling a fraction of the story. We must also remember that God has promised to decisively deal with the root cause of those instances of ugliness, namely, the sorts of tragedies instanced by these very illnesses. The sufferings are not limited to terminal illnesses alone. Illnesses for which cures are available here on earth will also be completely eliminated. Thus the healing we look forward to in heaven will be complete and final, ranging from healing of common colds to healing of cancerous tumors.

One of the most assuring promises of the end of suffering and the arrival of physical healing for all believers is the promise that death will be completely eliminated from our midst. The passage cited in the previous section makes this clear when it reminds us that there will be no more death or mourning or crying or pain. If we can find a way of alleviating death here on earth, we would all run for it; for no one really wants to die, unless, of course, the sufferings we go through turn out to be completely unbearable.

The experience of death is definitely a troublesome thing for all of us. Consider Michael Green's summary of different thinkers' views of the troublesome nature of death. Socrates observed that human hearts apprehend death to be the greatest evil. Albert Camus contended that it is the philosopher's only problem. Woody Allen, the atheistic movie star, said, "It is not that I'm afraid to die. I just don't want to be there when it happens." Francis Bacon, the philosopher of the Early Modern Period, noted that humans fear death as children fear to go in the dark.

The experience of death is therefore a troubling and a frightful one. Whereas it is true that believers need not fear death owing to the promise of a better life after death, it is still just as true that flesh, blood and bones cannot tolerate the inescapablwe arrival of death. Scripture does remind us of this inevitability. With equal certainty, though, it reminds us of the eventual elimination of death. It is a promise given to all believers. Jesus himself made this promise to Martha when he said, "I am the resurrection and the life. He who believes in me will live, even though he dies, and whoever lives and believes in me will never die. Do you believe this?"[22]

Jesus was fully aware of the troubling effects that death has on the emotions of the believer. Jesus himself was troubled by the death of Lazarus, his friend. Twice, we are told, Jesus was deeply moved: first, when he saw the mourning friends and relatives of Lazarus, and second, when he stood at the tomb of Lazarus. The original text uses words suggesting that Jesus was troubled by the suffering

---

22 John 11:25

that all human beings have to face. Notice that this suffering is the result of human sin. When God asked Adam, "Adam, what is this you have done?" he was really asking, "Do you really understand the seriousness of the consequences of your actions? Not only will you die, your offspring will die, all creation will suffer because of this rebellion on your part." Thus when Jesus was deeply moved, he was basically troubled by the kind of suffering that came as a consequence of human rebellion.

Notice also that Jesus was not only moved; he also wept. The fact that he wept and was moved are indications that he feels our pain, in spite of the fact that such pain and brokenness were things brought about by human rebellion in the Garden of Eden. The original text suggests that his being moved was an expression of his anger over the suffering that his creatures have to live through.

The fact that Jesus feels our pain raises an interesting point about deity. Theologians tell us that being God, Jesus is eternal. In other words, he is not constricted or bound by time. He is timeless. He thus has access to all of our situations in a timeless domain. If so, he has greater access to our pain more than we do – whether it is the sort of pain we experienced in the past or the kind we experience in the present. In other words, whereas we often go through moments of pain followed subsequently by some kind of healing, Jesus still feels our pain in a very real way. If Jesus, or for that matter, God, is all-knowing, his level of knowledge is deeper than any level we could imagine. This level of knowledge includes his awareness of the intensity of our suffering. He knows the pain we feel just as if he personally feels such pain. If he did not, he would not be omniscient. Hence he must feel our immediate pain as immediately as we do.

If it is in fact true that God does feel our pain, it is even truer that he suffers when we do. Otherwise, to use Professor William Dembski's words, he would be like a king or ruler quite unfamiliar with the struggles of his people.[23] We would like to think, on the basis of numerous passages from Scripture, that this would not be the kind of image we have of God. For example, the book of

---

23   William A. Dembski, *The End of Christianity: Finding A Good God in An Evil World* (Nashville: B&H Publishing Group, 2009), p. 19

Genesis presents God as being pained by the fact that he had created humans whose inclinations were toward wickedness. Also, the book of Isaiah presents Jesus as one familiar with grief and acquainted with suffering. In other words, he is the suffering servant.

Moreover, the very fact that Christ suffered on the cross is a clear indication that the Son of God knows what it means to go through pain. If Christ is an eternal being, a view that Scripture supports, we are here faced with a situation in which the suffering of Christ is as real today as it was when he hung on the cross. We know this for sure, in light of the fact that Revelation presents him as one whose robe was dipped in blood,[24] thereby underscoring the reality of Christ's memory of the crucifixion event.

If he indeed suffers when we do, the intensity of divine suffering must be more than any we can imagine, for it must necessarily include the sum of all human suffering, which of course is at his disposal in light of his omniscience. We humans cannot feel the sum of all human suffering, for we can only feel the pain we have been exposed to. God, however, feels the pain of all human beings put together.

Too often unbelievers complain, arguing that they cannot worship a God who allows bad things to happen to innocent people. How can God, for example, allow hundreds of thousands of people to die in devastating earthquakes like those witnessed in Chile, Haiti and Indonesia? Can he really be trusted with our lives if he allows those very lives to perish in natural disasters of the sort mentioned? Underlying such complaints is the assumption that God has no experiential knowledge of such human suffering. In other words, he merely is aware that his children suffer, but is totally indifferent to their suffering. By not acting to alleviate human suffering, they contend, he merely exposes them, on the one hand, to excruciating pain, some of them distributed in titanic proportions, while he, on the other, confines himself to some kind of a hedonistic paradise.

Of course this assumption is misguided, in light of what we have meditated upon above. God has not merely confined himself to a life of eternal bliss in heaven while remaining indifferent to

---

24 See Revelation 19:13.

human suffering. He is suffering along and together with his beloved creation. He knows their pain.

This implies something more pertinent to the passage we looked at above, namely, the promise that all tears, pain and death will be taken away. If God is truly a suffering being, he will want to do something to take away, not only the suffering he is experiencing, but also the suffering that his children and people are living through. The fact that his word promises to do away with such suffering is at least an assurance that his creation will find relief from pain. This in turn will take away the suffering that God has to go through when he watches his children suffer.

Thus believers have been promised a future life free of pain and suffering. Sicknesses, diseases, aches, death and pain will all be eliminated. A life free from such pain is surely to be desired for those who know what it means to suffer. Of course there are still issues about pain and suffering that we do not understand. For example, how is it that beings declared "very good" by God find themselves falling into a state of rebellion against God, thereby triggering moments of intense suffering? Various answers have been given to this question, one of them being that when God declared Adam and Eve "very good," he was referring to their structural goodness rather than to their moral goodness. However, since he created them with free will, their possibility of choosing to obey or not to obey him had to be very real. Otherwise their free will would not be free in a real sense. This is one of the many answers out there, and I believe it has some promise.

Be that as it may, what we do know is that every bad state that humans go through will be reversed, and that God will make everything right. In other words, God will replace every bad state responsible for human suffering with all good states that only God can offer. This then is part of the hope that every believer has, or should have, when faced with the reality of pain and suffering.

B. Healing from Emotional Suffering

I have discussed, quite briefly, the reality of physical suffering. More specifically, we have explored the kinds of sufferings we experience – sufferings brought about by the processes of nature. What I wish to examine in greater detail in this section is the reality of emotional suffering, which in many ways is closely related to and sometimes caused by physical suffering.

Roughly speaking, emotional suffering is perhaps understood as an individual's immediate awareness of an internal non-physical pain. In other words, the physical location of the pain is non-existent, but it is nevertheless there. Of course we use such expressions as "being wounded emotionally" or "being grieved at heart," and so on. These, however, are ways of trying to express the nature of non-material phenomena in terms denoting physical phenomena. This is not to deny the reality of emotional pain; on the contrary, it is an attempt to underscore its reality and distinctiveness from physical pain. In light of this, emotional pain is the sort of pain that cannot be immediately alleviated by the application of some medical procedure, though in some severe cases, therapy of a psychological or psychiatric nature may be necessary.

In earlier sections, I alluded to the passing on to glory of some of my closest friends. I also alluded, at the very beginning of this work, to my father's death. Needless to say, the death of these individuals close to me affected me deeply. In many ways I felt that my emotions were mortally wounded, though I could not quite individuate the physical location of the pain I felt. You will perhaps identify with me when I say that the emotional pain I felt were the sorts of pain I was hoping I could articulate in a way that would leave my listeners understand, in an intimate way, what I was going through. Part of the frustration came from realizing that none of my listeners understood me. I quickly discovered that this was normal, and that my failure to communicate my emotional pain was not unusual.

Christian psychologist Gary Collins seems to understand this when he writes the following words:

Grieving is never easy. We may try to soften the trauma by dressing up the corpse, surrounding the body with flowers or soft lights, and using words like "passed away" or "departed" instead of "died," but we cannot make death into something beautiful. As Christians we take comfort in the certainty of the resurrection, but this does not remove the emptiness and pain of being forced to let go of someone we love. When we encounter death, we face an irreversible, unalterable situation that we are powerless to change. Even though "death has been swallowed up in victory," the loss of a loved one can be devastating and grief can be overwhelming. Eventually, each of us will die, but in the meantime most of us will grieve at least periodically.[25]

One famous thinker went through a similar emotional experience that shattered his short terms dreams of enjoying marital bliss. I refer to C.S. Lewis, probably one of the most articulate defenders of Christianity in the nineteen fifties and sixties. Lewis wrote a book entitled *The Problem of Pain*, which was his attempt to make sense of God's goodness in light of the reality and facts of pain. One of his most famous lines in that book is his contention that pain is God's megaphone for rousing a deaf world.

As much of a masterpiece as that book was (and still is), it seemed that his articulations on the problem of pain, for the most part, took a back seat when he experienced the tragedy of losing his wife to cancer. This is not to indicate that Lewis abandoned his philosophy, or even his theology. Rather, the fact that he *made sense of pain* in that book provided very little comfort in the *reality* of the excruciating pain that he went through.

His book, *A Grief Observed*, was an articulation of his emotional roller coaster as he dealt with the reality of his wife's death. At some points in the book Lewis sounded visibly angry at God. In other instances any reader could almost feel his tears flowing freely. For example, Lewis wondered why, on the one hand, when we are so happy and with no sense of needing God, he still welcomes us when

---

25 Gary R. Collins, *Christian Counseling: A Comprehensive Guide*, Revised Ed. (Dallas: Word Publishing, 1988)p. 345

we turn to him; but on the other, when our need is so desperate, this very God slams the door on our face. "Why is God so present a commander in our time of prosperity and so very absent a help in time of trouble?"[26] Lewis asks.

To say that Christ faced the same things, in Lewis' view, fails to make it easier to understand why we go through what we do go through. In his view, the real conclusion in light of such suffering is not that God does not exist after all; rather, one realizes that this is what God is really like.[27]

Still, one would ask, are we prepared to believe in such a God, that is, the kind of God who allows his children to suffer? In light of this question, Lewis offers some penetrating insights, obviously gained from his painful experience. He reminds us, for example, that we never know how much we really believe anything until the truth of what we believe becomes a matter of life and death to us. Think about it in this way: it is easy for one to believe, for example, that a rope is strong and sound as long as one merely uses it to cord a box. However, if one were to hang by that rope over a cliff, then one would be forced to first discover how much one really trusted it. The insight he gains from this is summed up in the following contention: only a real risk tests the reality of a belief.[28]

To what extent, then, are we willing to believe that religion, or for that matter, Christianity, offers us much consolation in times of suffering? Lewis writes:

> Talk to me about the truth of religion, and I will listen gladly. Talk to me about the duties of religion, and I will listen submissively. But don't come talking to me about the consolation of religion, or I'll suspect you do not understand. Unless, of course, you can literally believe all that stuff about family reunions 'on the further shore.' But that is all unscriptural, all out of bad hymns and lithographs. There's not a word of it in the Bible.[29]

---

26   C. S. Lewis, *A Grief Observed*, HarperCollins Edition (San Francisco: HarperSanFrancisco, 2001), p. 5 – 6

27   Lewis, p. 6 – 7

28   Lewis, p. 22 – 23

29   Lewis, p. 25

For Lewis, then, the idea of reuniting with his wife, whom he refers to as H in his book, was perhaps not the kind of truth he was willing to embrace, at least not at that stage in his life. At the heart of his grief, he did not think Christianity provided much consolation.

To be sure, Lewis was skeptical about the absence of pain in heaven. Notice that such skepticism developed right when he was grieving the most. In the midst of his experience of pain, he did not think God could be trusted to keep humans from suffering even in the afterlife. To see how he reasons his way through this, consider his following observation. He says that if after H's death, she was now in God's hands, we must remember that H had been in God's hands all the time. Lewis believed that he had seen what God's hands did to H while she was still alive.[30] With regard to those very hands, Lewis asks:

> Do they become gentler to us the moment we are out of the body? And if so, why? If God's goodness is inconsistent with hurting us, then either God is not good or there is no God; for in the only life we know, he hurts us beyond our worst fears and beyond all we can imagine. If it is inconsistent with hurting us, then He may hurt us after death as unendurably as before it.[31]

Moreover, Lewis' temporary skepticism comes through quite forcefully when he contends that humans have no reason, by their own standards, to believe that God is good. According to Lewis, all the pieces of evidence suggest the exact opposite.[32] This is because, when God seems most gracious, he is really preparing the next torture. For Lewis, God has all the characteristics that humans call bad, including unreasonableness, vanity, vindictiveness, injustice and cruelty. In light of this, Lewis insists that we simply have no motives for obeying God. He writes: "If cruelty is good from God's

---

30 Lewis, p. 27

31 Lewis, p. 27 – 28

32 Lewis, p. 29

point of view, then telling lies may be good too. And what he calls heaven might well be what we should call hell."[33]

However, notice how Lewis begins to resolve these tensions. He gradually seems to come out of his skepticism, for example, by observing that the more humans believe that God hurts only to heal, the less they can believe that there is any use in begging for tenderness. This can be seen, for example, in our experiences with the surgeon at the operating table. Quite clearly, we would assume that the surgeon's intentions are good. The kinder and more careful he is, the more inescapably he will go on cutting. Hence, if he yielded to our pleas, all the suffering up to that point will be useless. From this true-to-life and realistic example, Lewis concludes that the existence of a good God makes these tortures necessary. Not even a moderately good Being could possibly bring them about if they were not necessary. Hence people who say they are not afraid of God because he is good have never been to a dentist;[34] for if we believe that a dentist, whom we are afraid of, is good and that his services are necessary, though very painful indeed, then by analogy we should also believe that if God is good, his shaping of our character is necessary, though very painful. Hence, just like we are afraid of the dentist, we should be even more afraid of God.

Whereas it is not exactly clear that Lewis completely overcame his grief, it would be safe to say, from reading that book, that some initial healing took place. For one, he did come to terms with the fact that the pain he went through, at the passing of his wife, had some minimal shaping of his character. Otherwise, he would not have spoken in a manner that drew analogies between God and a dentist.

Second, recall his claim that God slams the door shut on his children's face when they need him most. Apparently, Lewis seemed to go back on this claim in the following words: "Still, there are two enormous gains – I know myself too well now to call them 'lasting.' Turned to God, my mind no longer meets that locked door; turned to H, it no longer meets that vacuum – nor all that fuss about my

---

33 Lewis, p. 32
34 Lewis, p. 43

mental image about her."[35] Elsewhere he writes: "When I lay these questions before God I get no answer. But a rather special sort of 'No' answer. It is not the locked door. It is more like a silent, certainly not uncompassionate, gaze. As though He shook His head not in refusal but waiving the question. Like, "Peace, child; you don't understand."[36]

Third, consistent with his earlier claim that pain might just be God's megaphone to rouse a deaf world, Lewis asks us to imagine the following scenario. He asks us to think of the time when there was nothing in our souls except a cry for help. According to Lewis, such a time may be just the time God cannot give us such help. This is because we are like drowning people who cannot be helped because we clutch and grab. Perhaps our own cries deafen us to the voice (of God) we hoped to hear.

Thus, in a way, Lewis himself redeems his original contention, when he claimed that God was perhaps not as good as we thought he was. He begins to reconcile his view of God with the reality of suffering. For Lewis, suffering is real. It might call our belief in God's goodness into question. But if we understand suffering as God's way of shaping our character to make us more like him, then we will at least conclude that God is good.

I draw attention to Lewis' view of emotional suffering for the following reason. When Revelation 21:1-4 is fulfilled before our very eyes, the process of character building which Lewis talks about (quite briefly in *A Grief Observed* and more fully in *The Problem of Pain*) will be a reality for all believers. Pain, grief, sickness and death will no longer be necessary. In other words, there will be no reason for believers to live through these excruciating experiences. God will do away with them. For one, they came about because of human rebellion. Without desiring that they be a part of our lives, God still used them to bring us back to himself.

Since believers are saved from the penalty of sin, and are being saved from the power of sin, and will finally be saved from the presence of sin, the consequences of sin will be completely removed

---

35 Lewis, p. 61
36 Lewis, p. 69

from among God's children. They will then arrive at the final state of blessedness, which God had initially prepared for them before their rebellion in the Garden.

C. Healing of the Created Order

At the beginning of the first section of this chapter, I touched briefly on the healing of the earth in which God's children will no longer be victims of the devastation of natural disasters like hurricanes and tsunamis. In this section I want to explore more of this view. I alluded above to the healing brought about by God's people when they pray, seek his face and turn away from their wickedness. It is the sort of healing brought upon the land in which God's people dwell, healing that followed the devastating consequences of their sin.

It is not my intention to argue that God punishes sin today with such devastating consequences. There is no reason to believe that God no longer does this, and deciding whether he has or has not done so can be very tricky indeed. For this reason, I choose to postpone dealing with such issues to a different forum. The purpose of this forum, however, is to help restore hope to those devastated by tragedy and suffering.

Let me now turn to a familiar passage of Scripture, one I have already alluded to in earlier sections. I refer to the Apostle Paul's words in the book of Romans where he writes:

> I consider that our present sufferings are not worth comparing with the glory that will be revealed in us. The creation awaits in eager expectation for the sons of God to be revealed. For the creation was subjected to frustration, not by its own choice, but by the will of the one who subjected it, in hope that the creation itself will be liberated from bondage to decay and brought into the glorious freedom of the children of God. We know that the whole creation has been groaning as in pains of childbirth right up to the present time. Not only so, but we ourselves, who have

the firstfruits of the Spirit, groan inwardly as we wait eagerly for our adoption as sons, the redemption of our bodies.[37]

The Apostle Paul seems to be crystallizing for us a certain view of our redemption rarely spoken about in our churches – the view that all of creation will be redeemed. An alternative view suggests that this creation will be done away with, in fact, thrown away. It is the claim that a New Heaven and a New Earth will replace the one we have today. Such a view may have some merit. However, when we look at the original text, the presence of the prefixes, in the original text, seems to suggest a renewal of the current heaven and earth. Just as our bodies will be renewed, the earth we live in will also be renewed.

That the earth will be renewed is suggested by Paul's language in the text cited from Romans above. Notice his claim that the creation, it is hoped, will itself be liberated from bondage to decay, and brought into the glorious freedom of the children of God. The sense of this passage is that the current creation will in fact be liberated from its bondage to decay. It will be a refurbishing of sorts, done by God himself.

We must ask, though, what this 'bondage to decay' implies. We notice at once that the word decay is certainly not a very positive one. It denotes some kind of death, destruction, or perishing. Hence 'bondage to decay' seems to imply that creation has become a slave to death. However, it will be released, thereby becoming free from this slavery to destruction.

From Paul's description, then, we live in a world that decays. Its redemption from destruction will be brought about, presumably by God himself. Of course human beings are considered part of this creation, but we hardly think of other aspects of creation as redeemable. There is a sense in which the destruction we see in nature will no longer be there. In other words, except for God's creatures that have rebelled against him, God will bring about the

---

37
Romans 8:18 – 23

redemption of his entire creation, restoring it to its original state of fruitfulness.

This sort of restoration involves what we have already examined above, namely: the elimination of sicknesses, diseases, suffering, pain, death, destruction and so forth. When all these things are eliminated, we are certainly left with a created order full of tranquil such as has never been seen before.

Assume, for example, that something like our current technology will still be with us at our final redemption. Of course, theologically, this is quite likely a very flawed assumption, but it will definitely drive home the point I am trying to make. So I proceed gleefully. Assume, for instance, that we will have airplanes of the most sophisticated sort, equipped with the most sophisticated gadgets, far above the likes of our computerized radars and so on. In light of my mortal fear of flying, I am happy to report that in an earth redeemed by God, plane crashes will be completely unheard of (to be sure, it is extremely doubtful that we will even need planes). Foul weather will certainly not be a phenomenon any more – hence we will travel in a world free of deadly thunderstorms, whether on land or at sea.

This thought can be carried through into our day to day lives. If we will have automobiles in our newly refurbished earth, car wrecks will be a thing of the past. There will be no need for mechanics, or for car repairs or for replacements of gadgets. Everything will work as perfectly as intended by God. Perhaps, I hasten to note, we will no longer need cars because travel from one place to another will be of the most efficient sort.

Or think of a future world in which children are no longer dying of starvation brought about by failed rains or poor management of resources. It is a world in which there will be no need for relief efforts to better humanity, for humanity will have been perfected by God's saving grace. It is a world in which crops will yield in season, and they will do so consistently. If there will be any reason for farming, it will be because God will have ordained it in a way that will not demand painful labor or treacherous toil. It will be a world in which the earth will be completely healed to produce its crops and fruit just at the expected time.

More closely home, we will no longer be in need of hospitals, doctors, or nurses, in light of the fact that the natural processes that make it necessary for us to visit hospitals will be reversed. Sicknesses, aging and death will no longer be an issue. More accurately, sicknesses and diseases, having been eliminated in such a world, will make doctors and hospitals quite irrelevant.

Indeed, our future world would be quite a hopeless one if we will still see the need for doctors or the need for repairs in our homes, on our cars or on our roads. It will not be desirable if people will still die of hunger and starvation. There will not be much reason to look forward to such a world if natural disasters and calamities will still be a reality; for it will make no sense to replace this world with more of the same. In fact, if the future world will still be one in which sicknesses of any kind prevail, not much hope can we say is in store for Christians.

The reason we hope for a better world or for a better place is because we feel that something is terribly wrong with the one we live in. We feel that children should not die of starvation; people should not be killed by hurricanes, earthquakes and tornadoes; cancers should not invade our bodies; and so on. Perhaps this is the groaning of creation that the Apostle Paul discusses. It is a groaning that seems to express distaste for the condition of the current world – a protest of sorts.

At the same time, however, it seems to anticipate something better; and going by the promise of Scripture, we will not have more of the same in our future home in heaven as we do in the current one. It will be a healed world. In fact we will perhaps not know the full and true meaning of healing until we see that world. Everything that will be healed in that world will be healed perfectly and completely – that is, in the sense that they will not return to the bad states from which they were getting healed. I now turn to the healing of relationships.

D. Healing of Relationships

One of the most glorious experiences we will have in heaven is the joy of witnessing the healing of our relationships with one another. One of the most difficult things to come to terms with concerning our Christian fellowships here on earth is our inability to maintain healthy relationships with our families, friends, and those with whom we worship. It has been jokingly said that when we meet with God in heaven, that will be such glory. On the contrary, when we meet with friends here on earth, then Oh! What a story!

Whereas it should be clear that things need not be this way even here on earth, the fact of the matter is that they are. Church wrangles and fights seem to plague many Christian fellowships. Sibling rivalry is not a surprising phenomenon. Christians who cannot see each other eye to eye present a reality that embarrasses and hurts the body of Christ. The promise we get about heaven is that we will experience two kinds of healing in our relationships: first, heaven will bring about the healing of our horizontal relationships with one another. Second, heaven will bring about the healing of our vertical relationship with God.

Let's consider the first truth. Our hope of heaven comes with the promise of experiencing the healing of our horizontal relationships with one another. In heaven there will be no room, indeed, no place for fights, whether verbal or physical. Fighting believers who hope to enter God's heaven are well advised to reconsider their contentious spirit and adopt, for the wellbeing of their souls, a fully conciliatory disposition. This is true of all human relationships, including married Christian couples; fellowship groups that claim to identify with Christ; and all other groups that identify themselves as Christians. It would seem that at least all of the divisive and combative individuals will have to be called to answer for their ways (see Titus 3:10).

All this is to press the point that heaven is a place of healed relationships with one another. There will be no divorces in heaven. Of course there will be no marriages in heaven either. Neither will there be any broken relationships of the kinds we experience here on earth. Church fights and quarrels will be a thing of the past. In short, there will be peace and tranquility among God's children. This is because the presence and reality of God will unite all believers, and the very thing that causes fights and quarrels will have been removed from among God's people.

An important truth here, which seems to render the first truth even possible, is the contention that we will at long last experience the reality of the healing of our relationship with God. In the Garden of Eden, this relationship was broken by sin. At the Cross of Calvary, the relationship was restored by the death of Christ. However, when we enter the glory of heaven, the real meaning of this restored relationship will be powerfully impressed upon us. We will, for the first time ever, know by experience what it means to be loved by God. More than that, we will also discover just how much we can love our blessed redeemer. This is because the conditions for making it possible for us to be involved in our love for God will have been set in place by the very removal of sin from our natures.

Here on earth, we must admit that it is sometimes difficult to fully express our love for God. For example, many find it easier to sleep in than to rise early to have a quiet time with the Lord. In other instances some find it easier to stay at home than to drive or walk to church for a service that they suspect will be lacking in spiritual excitement. In many ways, it is difficult to be at least emotionally involved in loving a being that one, for the most part, does not see. In short, in much the same way that loving one another is hard work, truly loving God can be harder. Of course the hardness of this is brought about by sin.

Recall that we began to run away from God at the Garden of Eden. When sin entered the world through human choice on that enormously fateful day, it became harder and harder not only to see God, but to desire to be near God. Our loving God came looking for us, in spite of our rebellion. He more fully looked for us when his Son died on the cross. That was the significant starting point for the healing of our relationship with God, such that anyone who accepted Christ's offer of reconciliation would at once be spiritually healed. Despite the fact that we still sin even after accepting Christ's offer of reconciliation, we are at least assured of our eternal relationship with him.

Moreover, we hope and believe that someday sin will be removed from among us. When this happens, there is a sense in which we shall be restored and empowered to love God like we should. In other words, the conditions for loving God will be established by the removal of sin. In this way, the spiritual veil that keeps us from expressing delight in our Blessed Redeemer will be taken away, and we shall fully see God as he truly is.

In light of what we have said in these four sections, the believer in Jesus Christ has every reason to rejoice here and now. Hope for a better place in the future should enable one to live more fully in the present. When our future eternal destiny is seen in this positive and assuring light, we no longer see our sufferings as meaningless. This is because we know that in spite of their haunting presence, they will be eliminated, for they were brought about by a rebellion that will also be eternally purged from our midst in the final analysis.

Not only do we find meaning in our sufferings in light of this future and glorious hope. We find meaning in all other aspects of our lives as well. We find meaning in our trips to the grocery store, or in our exercise routines, in much the same way that we find meaning in our worship experience in God's temple – for our entire lives get centered on God given this perspective, in full knowledge that he desires the best for us rather than the worst.

Once again I recall a warning I made in the previous section. The promise of heaven and our desire to get there is not human centered. Rather, it is God-centered. In other words, we hope to enter heaven not for our own selfish reasons, but for the purpose of having a mutual enjoyment of our eternal relationship with him. Hence when we encounter God's divine healing in heaven, whether physically, emotionally, relationally, or from the perspective of the entire creation, we know at once that it is an act initiated by God to perfect us completely. This in turn enables us to have a perfect and eternal relationship with him. Heaven is therefore a place of eternal healing.

V. Heaven is a Place of Holiness

At the beginning of the last chapter, I noted that this is a broken world, evidenced by the many catastrophes and natural disasters that bedevil us every once in a while. Nowhere is this brokenness more evident than in the evils and atrocities that human beings bring upon their very own. It has been observed by many thinkers that humans are about the only species that kill their own.

There is some truth to this claim. Take, for example, the millions of Jews killed in the Holocaust. Not only do the numbers capture the horrific nature of the evils of that event; but the ways in which such deaths were carried out are extremely troubling. Indiscriminate executions of children and pregnant mothers in gas chambers and live furnaces has to leave the morally sensitive mind quite aghast at what the sinful nature in humans can do when left unrestrained. The mere fact that such events happened must leave the justice-starved human being to wonder whether this is in fact how everything will end.

Elie Wiesel, a survivor of the Holocaust, tells of his experiences in the hands of the Nazi while he was fifteen. Somehow, his family, along with other Jews, had been rounded up by the Nazis. The women were forcefully separated from the men during the roundup, and that was the last he saw of his mother and sister.[38]

As Wiesel and his father marched along, herded by the Nazis in the direction they quickly discovered was a crematory, Wiesel realized he would soon be burnt to ashes, along with his father. As they approached the burning furnace, they felt the heat from the crematory rising. In heart wrenching words, Wiesel wrote:

> We were gradually drawing close to the ditch, from which an infernal heat was rising. Still twenty steps to go. If I wanted to bring about my own death, this was the moment. Our line had now only fifteen paces to cover. I bit my lips so that my father would not hear my teeth chattering. Ten steps still. Eight. Seven. We marched slowly on, as though following a hearse at our own funeral. Four steps more. Three steps. There it was now, right in front of us, the pit and its flames. I gathered all that was left of my strength, so that I could break from the ranks and throw myself upon the barbed wire. In the depths of my heart, I bade farewell to my father, to the whole universe; and, in spite of myself, the words formed themselves and issued in a whisper from my lips: *Yitgadal veyitkadach shme' raha* ... May His name be blessed and magnified .... My heart was bursting. The moment had come. I was face to face with the Angel of death .... Two steps from the pit we were ordered to turn to the left and made to go into a barracks.[39]

What Wiesel witnessed was absolutely horrific. He saw human beings burnt alive, children among them. Obviously the experience left indelible images in his memory, for he wrote:

> Never shall I forget that night, the first night in the camp, which has turned my life into one long night, seven times cursed and seven times sealed. Never shall I forget the smoke. Never shall I forget the little faces of the children, whose bodies I saw turned

---

38 Elie Wiesel, *Night*, published as an excerpt in *The Problem of Evil: Selected Reading*, Michael L. Peterson, ed. (Notre Dame: University of Notre Dame Press, 1992), p. 79

39 Wiesel, p. 82 – 83

into wreaths of smoke beneath a silent sky. Never shall I forget those flames which consumed my faith forever. Never shall I forget that nocturnal silence which deprived me, for all eternity, of the desire to live. Never shall I forget those moments which murdered my God and my soul and turned my dreams to dust. Never shall I forget these things, even if I am condemned to live as long as God himself. Never.[40]

Whereas it is extremely difficult to read what Wiesel narrates here without wondering why God did not come to his family's rescue, one can imagine how much more difficult it must have been for him to witness the experience in person. Notice also the effect of that experience on his faith. On the one hand he is willing to walk into the flaming furnace offering a prayer that glorifies God. On the other, the experience is harsh enough, as he says, to consume his faith and murder his God. Without question, his belief in God took a beating. I intend to revisit this issue in greater detail below.

Meanwhile, let us look at a similar depiction of pain and suffering caused by human actions. I refer here to the suffering depicted by Fyodor Dostoyevsky. His book *Brothers Karamazov* is written in dialogue format, with Alyosha and Ivan presented as the main characters. At some point in their dialogue, Ivan contends that the innocent must not suffer for another person's sins. He believes that this is very true of children, given that children are so remote from grown-ups and hence, we could say, are of a "different species."[41]

However, notes Ivan, in spite of this self-evident truth, it is not always the case that children live pain-free lives. To prove his point, Ivan asks Alyosha to consider crimes, which he believed were committed by the Turks. Those crimes were done in fear of a general rising of the Slavs. Hence, they burnt villages, murdered and raped women and children. In fact they took pleasure in torturing children. Some of them cut unborn children from their mother's womb. Others tossed babies up in the air and then caught them

---

40 Wiesel, p. 83
41 Fyodor Dostoyevsky, *Brothers Karamazov*, published as an excerpt in *The Problem of Evil: Selected Readings*, Michael L. Peterson, ed. (Notre Dame: University of Notre Dame Press, 1992) p. 58

on the points of their bayonets right before their mother's eyes. In still another event, a trembling mother, knowing what was awaiting her baby, held that baby in her arms. A circle of invading Turks surrounded her. The Turks petted the baby and laughed to make her laugh. One of them pointed a pistol four inches from the baby's face. As the baby laughed with glee, it held out its hands to the pistol. The soldier then pulled the trigger in the baby's face and blew out its brains. All these, notes Ivan, gave zest to the amusement of the Turks.[42]

Another example that Ivan considers is the case of a Russian father, well-educated and quite a gentleman of sorts – at least according to the opinion of his peers. He and his wife beat their daughter of 7 with a birch rod, which was covered with twigs and thus stung more. With every blow he inflicted on his daughter, he was worked up to sensuality. He would beat her for over ten minutes, more often and more savagely. The child would scream until she could only gasp "Daddy!" several times. Interestingly enough, the case was brought to court, and a lawyer was engaged to defend the father. He argued, in his defense of the father, that this was a simple case of every day domestic event. He convinced the jury and the father was acquitted, as the public roared with delight over the acquittal.[43]

Ivan then draws our attention to another case of a Russian child – a little girl of 5, hated by her parents. The parents beat and kicked her for no reason. Her body was bruised all over. She was often shut up in a cold and frosty confinement. At night she needed to use the bathroom, but could not ask, perhaps for fear. Inevitably, she was forced to relieve herself *on* herself. The parents punished her by smearing her face with feces and made her eat it.[44]

Finally Ivan considers the case of a certain Russian general who punished a little boy for hurting his dog's paw. The general was of aristocratic connections. He retired from service into a life of leisure, and settled on his property and domineered over his poor neighbors.

---

42 Dostoyevsky, p. 59
43 Dostoyevsky, p. 61
44 Dostoyevsky, p. 62

He had kennels of hounds and nearly 100 dog-boys. One day a serf boy, about eight years of age, playfully threw a stone that hurt the paw of the general's dog. The general had the boy taken from his mother and had him locked up all night. The next day he summoned all his servants and dogs. He then got the boy's mother to stand in front of them all. The child was brought from the lock-up and was undressed. The general commanded the dog-boys to make the boy run. He then set the whole pack of dogs on the boy, tearing him to pieces before his mother's eyes.[45]

One cannot fail to sympathize with the cases that Ivan brings to our attention. They strike at the very fabric of our sensitivity to what we have come to term "innocent suffering," assuring us that something is indeed very wrong with human nature. This is where, as G. K. Chesterton reminded us, the doctrine of original sin is widely confirmed. However, besides merely retelling the story, it would be interesting to examine what Ivan had to say about these instances of human suffering, in which children had to suffer in the hands of their fellow human beings.

Ivan provides us with his rationale for taking up the case of children. He believes retribution for suffering must come now rather than later. Even if we must suffer to pay for eternal harmony, presumably, in heaven, Ivan wonders what innocent children have to do with this kind of suffering. He believes that it makes no sense for children to suffer to pay for eternal harmony.[46]

What Ivan concedes is the idea that it will in fact be great to finally see the justice of God when harmony (in heaven) comes. He believes that the mother will embrace the person that threw her son to the dogs. However, Ivan cannot accept that harmony. According to him, it is not worth the tears of the child who prayed to God for salvation; for those tears are un-atoned for. Revenge cannot atone for them. Neither will hell. Besides, if indeed there is a hell, argues Ivan, then there is no harmony.[47]

---

45 Dostoyevsky, p. 63
46 Dostoyevsky, p. 64
47 Dostoyevsky, p. 65

Ivan believes that harmony in heaven might just be an indication of divine justice. Despite this belief he still does not want the mother of the boy to embrace the oppressor who threw her son to the dogs. The mother dare not forgive the torturer, he insists. Ivan does not want harmony out of love for humanity. He would rather be left with the un-avenged suffering.

Ivan finally asks this rather penetrating question: suppose you create a fabric of human destiny. You aim to make humans happy in the end. Also, you aim to give them peace and rest at last; but to achieve this end, it was essential to torture a tiny child to death. Very penetratingly, Ivan asks, "Would you do it?"[48]

These are hard thoughts, with hard questions which must be answered. Let me begin with the thought raised by Wiesel. No doubt the experience he had was unimaginable. Only a person undergoing such an experience would know its negative impact on a person's emotions. The fact that Wiesel's experience consumed his faith is understandable if in fact this is the sort of world that God did not create.

We are also faced with the stories that Ivan brings to our attention. Ivan does not believe that heaven will ever atone for the suffering of innocent human beings. What then should we make of these two individuals who seem to have not only thought through these issues very seriously, but have also experienced them first hand? Do these experiences lead us to call God's existence into question, and subsequently abandon belief in him? I believe they do not, and here are a few reasons why.

First, God must not or should not be blamed for these experiences. As noted earlier in this work, sin is to blame. Recall my contention: God asked Adam and Eve that penetrating question after "discovering" that they had sinned against him. He asked, "What is this you have done?" God was really telling Adam and Eve, "You really do not understand the consequences of your actions. Your actions will bring about the breakdown of nature, the breakdown of the moral fabric of humanity, and the breakdown of your relationship

---

48 Dostoyevsky, p. 66

with me. Many will suffer because of this simple act of rebellion. The journey toward restoration will be a hard and painful one."

When sin entered the world through our forefathers, some of its consequences were, and still are, those of which Wiesel and Ivan spoke about in their writings. Clearly, those brutal acts that brought about the death of innocent children could not be attributed to morally upright people. The moral fabric of the society in which those innocent children were raised turned out to be extremely rotten. Therefore, God cannot be blamed for the suffering of innocent children. Sin is the culprit.

Closely tied to the first reason is the second one, namely: not only is sin to blame for these heart-rending sufferings and deaths of innocent children spoken about by Wiesel and Ivan; the perpetrators of those sinful acts ought to be blamed as well. In other words, both human beings and their sinful acts are to blame. Perhaps, in the midst of such painful tragedies, the appropriate question is not why God is doing nothing; rather, it should be why good people are doing nothing. One thinker reminded us that the only way for evil to triumph over good is for good people to do nothing. Whereas this is perhaps not true of every evil, it is certainly true of the kinds of evil spoken about by Wiesel and Ivan. In those situations evil would not have prevailed if God's good people did something to eliminate their occurrence.

Third, in the person of Jesus Christ, God has put frameworks in place for dealing with human evil. For one, he has made it possible, through the death of Jesus Christ, for humans to be redeemed from sin and its consequences. Hence, after personally defeating sin and its penalty by his death and resurrection, believers in him can confidently look forward to their final redemption from this evil world. To be sure, he has set aside a day when he will finally eliminate evil people who constantly reject his call to be holy.

This leads to the following implication, which forms my fourth point: Many evil people, (evil as defined by Scripture) seem to get away with their atrocities in this world. Perpetrators of the violence in Rwanda, Yugoslavia and the Holocaust all seem to have gotten away with their crime. For this reason we feel that justice has not been served; indeed we believe it will never be served if in fact a just God does not exist. However, we rest on the promise of Scripture that those who do evil will not get away with it. This includes those who burnt children at the Holocaust, the parents who beat their daughter senselessly and savagely and were later acquitted for it, and the general who set his dog on the poor innocent boy.

Not having the slightest sense of morality, and harboring an attitude of complete rejection of God, such people, if they indeed remain unrepentant and rebellious, have a clear destiny defined for them by Scripture: eternal life is not for them. Rather, they are headed for eternal damnation. Eternal life in heaven belongs to those who receive the saving grace of Christ and covenant to live holy lives. Instead the destiny of the aforementioned evildoer is destruction.

Heaven, on the other hand, is a holy place. Its inhabitants will be holy even as God himself is holy. True to Ivan's view, heaven will be a place of harmony. However, there is at least one problem with Ivan's view. He seemed to believe that even the general who set the dog on the poor boy will also be in heaven. If there is every indication that the general repented of his deeds, yielded to Christ's saving grace, and perhaps sought to set things right, as much as he could, with the boy's mother, then it would be reasonable to think that this general would in fact be in heaven, in much the same way, for example, that the Apostle Stephen is in heaven along with the Apostle Paul, Stephen's persecutor.

However, there seems to be no indication, from Ivan's part, that the general repented of his actions, or more importantly, that he embraced the saving grace of Christ. If he did not, then Ivan has no good reason to hold that harmony in heaven involves the unrepentant sinner enjoying the same eternal bliss with repentant and forgiven sinners. But Ivan does hold that this will be the case with the general.

For this reason, I find Ivan's theological view on heaven's inhabitants somewhat misleading. If I can cast doubt on the veracity of his view on heaven's inhabitants, which I believe I have done, we can also cast doubt on his contention that not even the promise of enjoying eternal life in heaven will right the wrongs done against innocent sufferers.

The fact of the matter is this: heaven will be a holy place, with a holy city, and holy inhabitants. The promise of the holiness of heaven gives us reason to believe that the evils that humans have suffered in the hands of their fellow human beings will be corrected. The holiness of heaven, in other words, gives us reason to believe that God is concerned about justice

A. Holiness of Heaven's City

The purity of the city in heaven is evidenced by the fact that the city is often described by Scripture as holy. A quick look at the twenty first chapter of the book of Revelation reveals this fact. For example, we find the following words in the twenty first verse: "I saw the Holy City, the new Jerusalem, coming down out of heaven from God, prepared as a bride beautifully dressed for her husband." Scrolling down to verse ten we read: "And he carried me away in the Spirit to a mountain great and high, and showed me the Holy City, Jerusalem, coming down out of heaven from God."

In both instances we read that heaven's city, the New Jerusalem, is a holy city. It is holy because it has been created for a holy purpose, namely: it will be inhabited by holy occupants – God's angels and God's redeemed saints. For this reason, we learn that the city will have no room for unrighteousness.

Michael Green's book gives us a clue to understanding this very notion of Holiness. In its attempt to explain holiness, we read the following words:

> What do we mean when we say a thing is holy? Look at your Bible and it says, "Holy Bible." What makes it holy? The land of Israel is called "The Holy Land," and the city of Jerusalem is called "The Holy City." Why? There is a quality about all three that they share in common. They all belong to God. The Bible is God's book; Israel is God's land; Jerusalem is God's city. They

are all God's property! That's why they are holy; they belong to God.[49]

Hence if we follow Michael Green's definition of holiness, we can say that the city in heaven is holy because it belongs to God. I do believe that an aspect of holiness is captured by this sense of 'belonging to God.'

The implication, of course, is that if something or someone seems to go contrary to God in some way, then generally speaking that thing or person in question is not holy. Another way to put it is as follows: if something or someone is set apart for purposes that clearly contradict God's intentions for our lives, then we look at a classic illustration of "unholiness."

To more adequately grasp this notion, compare the holiness of heaven with our earthly cities. It would be fair to say that most of the cities we live in have what we would call "the rough side of town." In such places one is advised not to walk late at night or alone or without some kind of security. Failure to take such pieces of advice into consideration places one's safety at risk. The assumption is that muggings, and perhaps robbery with violence, await the unsecured individual venturing into such places. This is because, it is argued, such places have bad characters notorious for doing drugs and engaging in dangerous gang activities. In such places, the presence of brothels indicates that prostitution is not uncommon, and that sexual immorality of all kinds, is the order of the day.

By comparison, a house of worship, like a church building or a chapel is revered for the very reason that it has been set apart for some sacred use. People go to such places to express their devotion and love to God, to confess their sin and right their relationship with God, and to worship God. Contrary to a brothel or a gentleman's club,[50] a house of worship is considered a holy place.

Of course this is not always the case for all churches. Whereas we believe that a church ought to be a holy place, a place of worship and confession of sin, some sins are notoriously difficult to eliminate

---

49 Green, p. 188
50 If the gentleman's club is what it is depicted to be, there seems to be nothing gentle about it.

among Christians. Having been a pastor for some time now, I am fully aware of this. To see this, consider the following humorous but, I admit, sad story depicted in Michael E. Hodgin's sermon illustration book.

> An old priest got sick of all the people in his parish who kept confessing adultery. One Sunday he said from the pulpit, "If I hear one more person confess adultery, I'll quit!"
>
> Well, everyone liked him, so they came up with a code word. Someone who had committed adultery would say they had "fallen."
>
> This seemed to satisfy the old priest, and things went well until the priest died. About a week after the new priest arrived, he visited the mayor of the town and seemed very concerned. The priest told the mayor, "You have to do something about the sidewalks in town. When people come to the confessional, they keep talking about having 'fallen.'"
>
> The mayor started to laugh, realizing that no one had told the new priest about the code word. But before he could explain, the priest shook an accusing finger at him and said, "I don't know what you're laughing about! Your wife fell three times this week!"[51]

As much as we want to assume that the church is a holy place, we still have instances of sin occurring in the body of Christ. Nevertheless, this does not negate one of the primary goals of the church, namely, a holy place in which God's people congregate to worship him.

Now, if a house of worship is somewhat revered for its holiness, then the holy city in heaven will be revered even more; for that is where our Most Holy God will fellowship with his redeemed saints. Exactly how this will happen is a reality too great to comprehend. The fact still remains, however, that the holy city will be more sacred

---

51   Michael E. Hodgin, *1002 Humorous Illustrations for Public Speaking* (Grand Rapids: Zondervan, 2004), p. 74

and more revered than any place of worship we will ever enter. We will have an unmistakable awareness of its holiness, one that will lead us to bow down and worship God with the highest honor and reverence we could ever muster in our finite human capacities.

In an earlier chapter, I discussed the beauty of that city quite at length. The fact of the matter is that once we set our foot in that city, besides the beauty that we will see before us, another aspect that will strike us about that city, with indescribable profundity, will be its holiness. If holiness were to be described in laundry terminology, the phrase "spotlessly clean" does not even begin to capture its purity. The city will therefore be both beautiful and holy.

It will be a city with no "rough streets" as is typical of earthly cities. Every corner of its streets will be safe. Every building in the city will be set apart for the glory of God. The city will have no brothels to defile its image. No ill-intentioned citizens will inhabit it to mug its citizens. Absolute purity will be its attribute. Addictive behavior like gambling, drunkenness and sexual immorality will have been purged from God's world, and only that which is holy will be close to God. The beauty and holiness of that city will be such that everyone, including the wicked, will desire to be a part of it, but only the redeemed will enjoy it. This now leads us to the next truth, namely: the citizens of heaven will be holy.

B. Holiness of Heaven's Inhabitants

Toward the end of the lengthy introduction of this chapter, I alluded to the fact that unrepentant evil men and women will have to be called to account for their deeds. The Bible is clear that such individuals will not in any way enjoy eternal life in heaven with God. This is because heaven has been set aside for holy inhabitants.

We must bear in mind that God has specific standards set in place. Those standards cannot be compromised. They are standards specifying how we ought to live. However, the painful reality is that we fall short of those standards. It is only through the saving grace of Christ that we can be justified before God. This has been the Gospel message since the early church began its evangelistic enterprise.

What strikes us as interesting, in light of this reality, is the fact that the world we live in is somewhat hostile to this understanding of the world. The moral code outlined by Jesus Christ is never embraced with good cheer in the secular world. For one, this moral code does make some very specific demands, requiring a radical change of behavior and attitude, a change the secular world finds quite burdensome.

In light of this, let us face some honest truths about this. The so-called "burdensomeness of the laws of Christ" is not exactly that at all and therefore quite misleading. Christ's laws are meant to protect us from the kind of downward spiral typical of immoral actions that humans often face. The reality presented by Christ's laws can be captured by two options: either we choose to obey Christ's laws and experience eternal enjoyment of a joyous life and unending happiness in heaven, or we opt for the addictive patterns of sinful living followed by its destructive consequences in the end. These are the only two options. There are no middle grounds.

Of course one might object and say that some people have lived morally good lives without having to pay due respect to God's laws and rules. They hate no one. They do not commit adultery. They do not steal. They do none of these things; and such people are not Christians either. They are honorable members of our society. We must therefore say that for as long as we can imagine this scenario as a possibility, then it is quite possible to live a moral life without paying homage to the message encapsulated by Scripture.

This objection sounds like a possible scenario, one that we can envision. However, if we go with what Scripture tells us, we learn that all have sinned and fall short of God's glory. In other words, there is no one righteous, not even one (See Romans 3:11 – 23). We constantly violate God's law and fall short of his ways.

Even without falling back on the Bible, the fact that we have all sinned, or broken some moral code, is not difficult to see. Consider the words of Christ as an illustration of this. Christ reminds us that if any man looks at a woman lustfully, that man has already committed adultery with that woman in his heart. In light of this claim, we must be led to confess that all men (as opposed to women) are adulterous.

Almost at the risk of making a sweeping statement, there is not one man that has passed this test. If this is the case, then all men are sinners. I do not know that women are exempt from this either.

Moreover, we do not want to limit this to the sexual arena, since that is not the only arena in which our self-deception about our own morality can be exposed. There exists also the question of hate. At one time or another we find ourselves hating some people and loving others. I know of no one who succeeds in loving everyone equally, except, of course, Jesus alone. It might be that there is at least one other than Christ. I doubt, however, that such a person will not be offended by somebody in the near future in a way that causes the root of bitterness to spring up in the person.

Or take the case of anger. The person who never gets angry is no human being. Anger is a normal part of our lives. There is a kind of anger that turns out to be sinful, one that seems tantamount to murder. We get angry at each other. Some things offend us to the extent that we feel the urge to revenge. That tendency to be vengeful, which resides in all of us, is in violation of God's law.

One of the most intuitive cases is in the area of telling the truth. It is safe to say that no human being tells the truth all the time. It is doubtful that we will ever find a person who has never told a lie from birth, even if we do so in non-serious situations. We have all told at least one lie at one time or another in our lives. Hence, it is extremely difficult, perhaps impossible to find someone who has lived a morally impeccable life of the sort our objection cited above is trying to allude to.

The point of what I am saying is this. Moral uprightness is not something limited to human action alone. Moral uprightness is a matter of the heart. As we have always been reminded by theologians, the actions we perform do not make us sinners. We perform those actions because we are sinners already. In other words, deeply ingrained in our being is the tendency, indeed, the inclination, to sin and violate God's laws.

Put differently, there exists a beast in each one of us. We are capable of committing some of the most atrocious crimes this side of heaven. All this is to underscore the fact that there are no middle grounds for being moral. We either go the way of the Gospel of Christ that transforms the human heart from the inside so that morality becomes a way of life for us, or go the way of worldly patterns of morality – a way that enslaves us to utter destruction. No one in his or her sanity really wants to choose a path of eternal destruction. It is therefore only logical that we should choose a life of obedience to Christ and reap the benefits of enjoying this life eternally with God.

What does this kind of life, eternal life with God, truly entail? For our part, it would entail, first of all, a full realization of our inability to attain any righteousness on our own that would get us to our eternal destiny. Second, it would also entail admitting that only Christ's death on the cross for our sins made it possible for us to enjoy this life. In short, it is a gift given to us by God, such that once we accept that Christ paid the penalty for our sins, and turn to him in repentance, he will cleanse us from our unrighteousness, and open the door for us to enjoy an eternal and joyful relationship with him in heaven.

Now that we have reasonably established that we are all sinners in need of forgiveness, and that such forgiveness is possible only by Christ's atoning death on the cross, and that this death will make it possible for us to enjoy eternal life in heaven with God, let us now turn to Revelation 21:7, which reads:

> He who overcomes will inherit all this, and I will be his God and he will be my son. But the cowardly, the unbelieving, the vile, the murderers, the sexually immoral, those who practice magic arts, the idolaters and all liars – their place will be in the fiery lake of burning sulfur. This is the second death.

Another passage puts it succinctly thus: "Nothing impure will ever enter it, nor will anyone who does what is shameful or deceitful, but only those whose names are written in the Lamb's book of life." [52]

Both texts make it clear that those who have not been purified, or for that matter, saved by Christ's atoning death on the cross will not enjoy eternal life made available to God's children. Or put differently,

---

52 Revelation 21:27

those who consistently and rebelliously reject God's call to holiness and Christlikeness will painfully miss this wonderful opportunity to spend eternal life with God. Eternal life is for everybody that trusts in Christ as his Lord and Savior. More accurately, eternal life is meant for those whose lives have been sanctified by Christ's atoning death on the cross. The inhabitants of heaven will therefore be holy individuals, irrespective of whether we are speaking about humans or angels. This is because the designer of heaven is himself holy.

Let's begin with human beings who will inhabit heaven. As we think of heaven, and particularly of the New Jerusalem, we are thinking of a city whose inhabitants will pursue all the virtues that reflect lives of holiness. The implications of these are quite enormous. In the previous section, I discussed quite considerably, the implications of a holy city. Let me now pursue that thought with respect to humans who will have been purified and who will also inherit eternal life in heaven.

Inhabitants of heaven will live in safety. They will live in harmony. They will also enjoy a life of peace and tranquility never before experienced in the history of humanity. Wars and conflict will be unheard of. The sorts of human-caused evil that we read about in the news will all be eliminated. There will be no more crises like the ethnic cleansing witnessed in the Holocaust, or in Rwanda, or in Yugoslavia. Rape, murder, theft, and other forms of violence will not only be completely eliminated from the saved and sanctified society. They will also be forgotten; for we are told that we will be saved from the presence of sin on that day. Hence the things we fear most that could ever be inflicted on us by our fellow human beings will be gone.

The holiness of the inhabitants of the city does not imply only the absence of violence. It also implies the elimination of non-violent immoral acts as well. Things like drug addiction, drunkenness, alcoholism, lying, witchcraft and all forms of sexual immorality, will no longer plague individuals who wish to live holy lives forever with their Lord.

Hence believers in Christ look forward to safe city streets, without drive-by shootouts and violent gang activities. They look forward to drug free environments and orgy-free neighborhood parties. They look forward to peaceful coexistence with each other, loving neighborhoods and simple happy interactions with one another. It will be a society that no earthly human community will ever succeed in foreshadowing; for this will be a neighborhood designed by Christ himself.

Let me now proceed to other inhabitants of the city. I refer here to angelic beings. The Bible has quite a bit to say about angels. For one, we do know that some of them are God's messengers. Others, called the cherubs and seraphs, seem to have a specific ministry around the throne of God. We also know that they are spiritual beings. Those designated as God's messengers usually perform specific tasks among humans or convey specific messages to human beings. Sometimes, as in the case of Daniel, they deliver answers to prayer. In other cases, they intervene to deliver humans from imminent disaster, when, for example, the angel warned Joseph and Mary, telling them to flee to Egypt in order to save the life of the Baby Jesus. In other instances, they are involved in spiritual warfare, fighting against the devil for God's cause.

It appears that angels will also be citizens of that Holy City in heaven. Whereas we do not know exactly how angels really look like, the Bible seems to indicate that they are extremely powerful beings – and they have to be if they must be involved in the sort of spiritual warfare mentioned every now and then in Scripture. We also know by scriptural records that their appearances are nothing short of dazzling such that we immediately feel a sense of dread when we countenance them.

However, these dazzling, powerful but friendly beings will be our neighbors in the holy city, so to speak. How we will interact with them is quite unknown, though I believe it will be one of the most fascinating things that we will experience in heaven. Perhaps we will discover that some of them knew us all along, and were perhaps alongside us as we lived our lives here on earth. It is also possible that we will communicate with them in the same way that we communicate with one another. It is even more possible that some of the unanswered questions about our suffering and pain will be settled when we speak with them. However, I hasten to add that all our answered questions about our suffering and pain and evil will be fully settled by God himself, for he will be the one to wipe away all our tears.

Most of what I say about the angelic beings is only speculation on my part. At any rate, we will be aware of their holiness as we live with them. This holiness will be one of the most attractive things that we will ever experience in that holy city. The joy of living alongside these beings, and the anticipation that comes along with it should make our hearts race with excitement. Perhaps it is for this reason that the Bible says, "No eye has seen, no ear has heard what the Lord has prepared for those who love him." Indeed, what has been prepared for us must leave us wondering why we do not have as many people believing in the Lord Jesus Christ.

For this very reason, I wish to underscore one point: those who reject the saving grace of Christ are missing out on the greatest experience any human being will ever have. A life in heaven is such a precious gift given to us that no human being should give it away in exchange for a life of eternal damnation. Not even the hymn *When We All Get to Heaven* begins to fully capture what we shall experience in that wonderful home prepared for us. We will have an opportunity to live a pain-free and sin-free life. We will gaze on the beauty of God forever and ever, and will never get bored with what we see; for that beauty and holiness will be eternal, never-ending. Let me now turn to the holiness of God.

C. Holiness of God

God is as Absolutely Holy as he is Absolutely Beautiful. I said earlier that when we cross over to the other side, one of the first things to strike us with unforgettable profundity will be the Absolute Beauty of God. Now that we are discussing God's holiness, allow me to modify that claim. It will not just be the Absolute Beauty of God that will strike us with such great impact; what we will see before us will also be a being of Absolute Holiness. Think about it in this way. Only God can be Absolutely Great and Absolutely Beautiful and Absolutely Holy simultaneously. This is such that the being you will see before you, once you set your foot in heaven, will be as Great as he will be Beautiful as he will be Holy. Of course these are not his only attributes. However, no other being can posses even one of these attributes in the intrinsic sense.

As we consider the subject of God's holiness, I am immediately aware of my inability to expound on this topic for the simple reason that any attempt to describe God's holiness is severely limited not only by human language, but also by human sin. With regard to human language, God's holiness is surely indescribable. This is not to say that it is nonsensical; rather, it is an admission that words are incapable of conveying the facts of God's holiness. With regard to human sin, we are hindered by our spiritual defects to truly and fully grasp what God's holiness truly entails. This is an admission similar to the one I made when describing, not only God's greatness, but also God's beauty.

This endeavor is not entirely futile, though. I believe that we can somewhat come to an understanding of God's holiness, which though severely limited, can still be useful in providing us with implications for living our lives. Our sourcebook for this, of course, is Scripture. We will look at specific events in the Bible that talk of God's holiness – events that capture the reaction of those blessed with the experience of countenancing God in his splendor and holiness. I begin with the passage from Isaiah 6:1 - 5 that reads:

> In the year that King Uzziah died, I saw the Lord seated on a throne, high and exalted, and the train of his robe filled the temple. Above him were seraphs, each with six wings: With two wings they covered their faces, with two they covered their feet, and with two they were flying. And they were calling to one another:
>
> "Holy, holy, holy is the Lord Almighty; the whole earth is full of his glory."
>
> At the sound of their voices the doorposts and thresholds shook and the temple was filled with smoke. "Woe to me!" I cried. "I am ruined! For I am a man of unclean lips, and I live among

a people of unclean lips, and my eyes have seen the King, the Lord Almighty."

For some reason, Isaiah is blessed with the experience of seeing a worship service going on in the temple in heaven. God's angels repeatedly proclaim God's holiness to one another, proclaiming that the whole earth is full of God's glory. Also, we read of how Isaiah is immediately impacted by God's holiness, and of his reaction to it. Worth noting is the fact that when Isaiah saw God's holiness, he became aware of his own sin.

The following story, though obviously very limited, helps to give us an idea of what is going on here. Several years ago, a friend of mine happened to walk into a prestigious restaurant in a certain city. The friend was fairly decently dressed – at least that is what he thought. What he did not know is that he walked into a restaurant that was frequented by the region's dignitaries. To say that those dignitaries were smartly dressed is an understatement. They all seemed to wear the latest designs in fashion industry. This friend, though decent, was clad in a pair of pants and a shirt, which he bought from a local store. He looked seriously underdressed among those dignitaries. As soon as his eyes fell on the occupants of the restaurant and their latest-of-fashion designs, he was immediately aware of his wardrobe short comings. Under normal circumstances, he looked great. Nevertheless, set against the view presenting itself before him, he felt completely out of place.

I believe something analogous to this is what Isaiah felt. It is perhaps not the central idea in this passage. However, consider that by his own standards, Isaiah probably did not think he was sinful enough to deserve the death sentence. Once he saw Ultimate Holiness right before his eyes, though, he knew he was in trouble. How could a person as sinful as he was set eyes on the Most Holy and live! Something about God's holiness struck him with indescribable dread. He felt he was unworthy to have his unholy eyes countenance the holiness of God.

Jones Kaleli, professor of missions and intercultural studies at Liberty university puts it well. According to him, it is conceivable, perhaps, that at that moment Isaiah had a little glimpse as to why the sinless angels never dared to have their eyes countenance the holiness of God. The one indwelt by absolute holiness, notes Kaleli, is the one in whose presence the sinless angels must use two of their wings to cover their faces as they called, "Holy, holy, holy is the Lord Almighty." We must therefore think that at his presence, human saints as cleansed sinners can only bow down in adoration.

Many more passages of Scripture either describe directly or imply, in some indirect way, the holiness of God's throne such that the beholders of this lofty view find themselves falling face down simultaneously acknowledging God's greatness and sensing their unworthiness before God. For example, in the first chapter of Ezekiel, the prophet discusses the majesty of the scene before him and the effect it had before him thus:

> Then there came a voice from above the expanse over their heads as they stood with lowered wings. Above the expanse over their heads was what looked like a throne of sapphire, and high above on the throne was a figure like that of a man. I saw that from what appeared to be his waist up he looked like glowing metal, as if full of fire, and that from there down he looked like fire; and brilliant light surrounded him. Like the appearance of a rainbow in the clouds on a rainy day, so was the radiance around him. This was the appearance of the likeness of the glory of the Lord. When I saw it, I fell facedown, and I heard the voice of the one speaking.[53]

The point I wish to press in this passage is simply this: when confronted by the holiness of God, we feel a sense of inadequacy, a sense of absolute smallness. Similar sentiments are expressed by the Apostle John in the following passage:

> I turned around to see the voice that was speaking to me. And when I turned I saw seven golden lampstands, and among the lampstands was someone "like a son of man," dressed in a robe reaching down to his feet and with a golden sash around his chest. His head and hair were white like wool, as white as snow,

---

53 Ezekiel 1:25 – 28

and his eyes were like blazing fire. His feet were like bronze glowing in a furnace, and his voice was like the sound of rushing waters. In his right hand he held seven stars, and out of his mouth came a sharp double-edged sword. His face was like the sun shining in all its brilliance. When I saw him, I fell at his feet as though dead.[54]

In all these instances, when the perceivers somehow became aware of the holiness of God, they found themselves falling down, demonstrating an awareness of being too unworthy to behold what was presenting itself before them, or more accurately, acknowledging that what they saw was way beyond the ability of their cognitive faculties to handle. By doing this very thing, they also admitted that the being they saw before them was so lofty that they found themselves bowing down either in a posture of worship or almost in a state of worship.

Notice that this experience is true not only for beings living on earth. It seems to be true for beings in heaven as well, the sorts of beings that the book of Revelation refers to as the twenty four elders. When they come before the presence of God's holiness, it has the impact of leading them to fall before him. The passage in question reads:

Each of the four living creatures had six wings and was covered with eyes all around, even under his wings. Day and night they never stop saying:

"Holy, holy, holy is the Lord God Almighty, who was, and is, and is to come."

Whenever the living creatures give glory, honor and thanks to him who sits on the throne and who lives for ever and ever, the twenty-four elders fall down before him who sits on the throne, and worship him who lives for ever and ever. They lay their crowns before the throne and say:

---

54 Revelation 1:12 – 17a

"You are worthy, our Lord and God, to receive glory and honor and power, for you created all things, and by your will they were created and have their being."[55]

We see then that even with other holy beings in heaven, worship of God because of his holiness comes spontaneously. It is safe to say that this cognitive "seeing" of God's holiness, then, is what will punctuate our worship of God when we finally see him face to face. Not only shall we be aware of our inadequacy; we will also find ourselves acknowledging his greatness. These seem to be key ingredients of worship: acknowledging that God is too great for our cognitive faculties to handle, and that we are too small to behold him, yet by his grace he has allowed us to see him as he is and to have that deep and eternal relationship with him.

As noted earlier, it is extremely difficult to describe God's holiness. We do know, though, that when we finally see him in the beauty of his holiness, our worship of him will be spontaneous. It will be infinitely more spontaneous than seeing a beautifully drawn picture and finding ourselves responding with a big "wow." It will be infinitely more spontaneous than seeing a beautiful play in a ball game and standing up to applaud the athlete. It will be infinitely more spontaneous than listening to beautiful praise music or Handel's *Halleluiah Chorus* and finding ourselves rising and lifting our hands in praise and adoration.

One speaker captured this concept in this way: If the mayor of our city walked into a meeting hall filled with citizens, the citizens will all rise and give him a round of applause. If the governor of that state walked into the same hall, the citizens will quite likely do the same, rising and giving him a round of applause. In fact, if the president of that country walked into the room, there will be pomp and music, and all will rise to give him a louder round of applause. However, when Jesus Christ, the King of Kings steps into any room, all will fall down and worship him; for what they will see will not be the worship of a mayor, or the grace of a governor, or the excellence of a president. What they will see will be the Absolute Holiness of God!

---

55   Revelation 4:8 – 11

VI. Heaven Is A Place of Answered Questions

We have seen the many exciting aspects of heaven that believers will enjoy when they finally get there. We have seen, for example, that heaven is a place of greatness, namely, that believers will be endowed with the sort of greatness that no human has ever witnessed. We have also seen that heaven is a place of beauty, once again determining that believers will have a cosmic transformation that will be nothing short of glamorous. Another aspect that we have considered is the idea that heaven will be a place of eternal healing. Believers will witness the healing of their bodies, they will live in a healed "land" and their relationship with God will also be healed. Fourth, we have discussed the view that heaven is a place of holiness. We have seen that without holiness no one shall see God. We have also seen that when we set eyes on God, we will find ourselves, spontaneously, bowing down to worship him.

I now want to move on to something related to the previous four chapters, that hopefully helps to tie together everything I have hitherto said, namely, that heaven is a place of answered questions. In other words, I want to explore the view that in heaven all the questions we have ever raised or will ever raise in this life concerning things we did not understand about God, life, salvation, meaning, suffering, and so on, will be answered.

I have often heard many Christians say, "When I get to heaven, I will want to know the answer to such and such a question." I heard this type of remark both in Bible School and in Seminary. Very little has changed since then. Professors and students alike seem to have questions which, they feel, need to be answered. As a seminary professor, I still have unanswered questions, questions whose answers seem hitherto unavailable.

How do we know that such questions cannot be answered? A theological question whose answer is unavailable here on earth is the sort of question whose answer the Bible is silent about, or at least seems to be silent about and whose answer philosophy seems incapable of answering. To be sure, philosophy is precisely what it is because it merely asks questions rather than solve them. A philosopher can always settle an issue for himself or herself, but it is doubtful that once settled in this way, other philosophers and thinkers find those answers satisfactory. Notice that even this aforesaid view is open to question, thus proving my point!

I note all this in order to point out that human beings ask profound questions. For some of those questions, the answers will never be available this side of heaven. They are the sorts of questions, for those of us who believe in heaven, that only heaven will be able to answer. In other words, only when we meet with our Lord face to face shall we be able to find answers to questions that we could not answer in this life.

I believe, for example, that many of our questions about human suffering will be comprehensively answered in heaven. Irrespective of the many theodicies that try to make sense of God's existence in light of the facts of suffering, there are still some questions that are left unanswered, even for believers. The unanswered questions, however, are not enough to cause believers to abandon their faith. They merely make us see that belief in a God that can be trusted is really and more truly a matter of faith than a matter of anything else.

Let us look at this issue more intimately. Believers have been promised that everything will be made right by God in the final analysis. As we live our lives in the present, all the pieces of evidence seem to point to the contrary. For example, people still die. Sicknesses become more and more sophisticated, with viral resistance to drugs becoming more and more evident. Moreover, if you have read this far, you will recall that natural disasters are becoming more and more common. This leaves us wondering whether we are in any way heading toward a restoration of all things, or whether we are in fact plummeting to eventual destruction of the universe.

Various responses can be made here. One response, for example, is to assume that everything will get worse and will never get better precisely because this is the pattern we see, and that it is a pattern consistent with important scientific principles. There is also an alternative response, namely, that things will eventually get better despite evidence to the contrary. More specifically, they will get worse before they get better. This seems to be the view endorsed by Scripture. Jesus did warn us that there will be wars, rumors of wars, earthquakes, famines, ethnic tension and so on. The warning does not stop there. Jesus went on to tell us that these are the beginning of birth pains. Put differently, these are just the initial stages of the last days. They will get more severe as the last days approach.

Of course, this view of Scripture has been abandoned by the so-called free-thinkers. They have walked out on God on the basis of what they think is impeccable evidence against his existence. By doing so, they believe they make an intellectually satisfying move. This is something we see time and again from former believers in God, as well as from non-believers who start off as earnest seekers of truth, but end up rejecting the faith because they find its postulations quite difficult to handle. I think, however, that this walking away is happening carelessly, and for that matter, prematurely.

By way of illustration, imagine you are watching a movie in a movie theater. As the plot of the movie thickens, you begin to dislike the direction it is taking. For example, you feel angry that the bad guys in the movie are having the upper hand, thereby prevailing over the good guys. It reaches a point where you see no logical way in which the good guys will ever score so much as a single victory over the bad guys. Hence, before the movie is over, you walk out on it and conclude it was a very bad movie.

Much later, a friend of yours that goes to the same theater to watch that very movie with you, stays right through the movie, sees the end, and comes home feeling satisfied that it was one of the best movies he ever saw. He then tells you how it ended, how the good guys finally overcame the bad guys, and how the many things you overlooked as the plot advanced turned out to contribute to the final victory of good over evil. At that point you immediately discover how you prematurely jumped to unwarranted conclusions about the movie, conclusions you would not have embraced had you been open to allow the movie's plot to develop.

I believe that something like this is going on among the unbelievers of our current generation. They walk away on God because they believe that God's existence cannot be reconciled with the facts of suffering. They seem to conclude, before the unfolding plot of the universe is over, that suffering and pain is prevailing over our well-being, and that this can only be the case in a world uncreated by God. However, as the illustration above has shown, just because God does not seem to be doing something to alleviate our suffering immediately does not mean he is doing nothing at all.

It is quite possible, for example, that God is working behind the scenes perhaps in ways we can neither understand nor imagine. It is for this reason that the question of faith and trust in God becomes crucial. We need to trust his ways and methods of doing things. It is quite possible that this working behind the scenes is not only his way of working to stop our suffering, but that it is also the best and only way for him to stop our suffering.

Hence, walking away on God at this stage would be tantamount to walking out of the movie theater before the movie is over. This then becomes a premature and careless way of responding to a God who has urged us to trust him well enough to deal with our suffering. We would thus be well advised to be patient with God in this regard; for after all, God himself is patient with us in our weakness. If he were to walk out on us for our failure to deal with our own internal evil and sinful choices, we would be the first ones to complain. We would scream from the top of our lungs that we need time to work on our weaknesses. In all fairness, then, God is asking us to be patient with him as he works the fabric of our universe in order to alleviate our suffering.

The stage that is our world is like a movie whose script is rolling along. We have not arrived at the final scene yet, though we are steadily moving in that direction. If we give up on God at this time, we will be making a premature decision. If we remain faithful to him, we will not only be blessed with seeing the final triumph of God over suffering and evil; we will also delight in arriving at the answers to some of the biggest questions we have asked in our lives here on earth.

With regard to suffering and pain, it will finally be clear to us why a good and loving God allowed us to suffer the way we did. In many ways we will discover that it was precisely because he is a loving God that he allowed us to suffer in significant ways, and that the experience itself would make us love God even more. Also, perhaps we will be able to understand, in a very real way, how God himself suffered in the person of Jesus Christ, and the excruciation involved in having God forsake his own Son at the cross. I believe that that event was just as painful for God the Father as it was for God the Son. In addition, perhaps we will also understand that God himself was more concerned about stopping our suffering than we ever were, and that he did more than we could ever imagine either to reduce the intensity of our suffering or to enable us to go through that experience patiently. Hence heaven will be a place where our unanswered questions here on earth will finally be settled.

There are broader issues that every human being seems to be concerned about besides the whole question of suffering. Many religious thinkers identify at least five areas in which human beings ask fundamental questions of life, namely: the areas of origin, morality, meaning, identity and destiny. These areas define questions that human beings in all cultures have tried to answer. With slight variations, Christian thinkers, apologists and pastors have tried to explain how the Bible answers these questions consistently and satisfactorily, at least in a way that appeals to our being as created entities. Whereas non-believers still question the believer's answers to these questions, the hope of heaven enables us to see that the questions wrought by these five areas will be decisively answered. Let's begin with the first one.

A. Heaven's Answer to the Question of Origin

When I was about four years old, I remember asking my mother that all-too-often-brushed-aside question, namely, "Where did I come from?" My mother, being the taboo conscious lady that she was then, and still is to this day, answered by telling me that she felt an irresistible urge to throw up, which she did, and out I came. I then asked her why she did not throw up more of us so I could see how it was done. I wondered if I could do the same too.

As humorous as this story might sound, allow me to suggest that we all ask this question of origin at one time in our lives. We want to know how we got here. Philosophers have taken it to the next level, asking, "Why is there something rather than nothing?" This is because we realize, from everyday experience, that physical objects, including human beings, do not just pop into existence without a cause. We feel that something caused our existence, that we are here because of the actions of some prior, or if you like, proximate causes.

I come from a background that has numerous stories of how we got here. Quite interestingly, most of those stories seem to trace their origin back to a Divine Being, which most believed compared in interesting ways to the God of the Bible. Trying to explicate the nature of those stories at this point would take us far afield. What I want to underscore, however, is the very fact that we all feel that the existence of this universe calls for some explanation. For most believers, atheist Bertrand Russell's explanation is unacceptable; for he argued that the universe just happens to exist, and that's it.

We also have different naturalistic explanations, one of them being the view that the universe is eternal, that it has always been there. Since the discovery of what scientists call the Big Bang, the view that the universe is eternal is becoming less and less popular among scientists. Even with the alternative explanation of the Big Bang, we must wonder as believers, what caused the Big Bang. Reason seems to tell us that the Big Bang is not something that just happened spontaneously without prior causes triggering the event.

The Bible gives us a different explanation. It maintains that the universe was caused by a Divine Being – a being that is itself uncaused. This being, maintains the Bible, is eternal and exists outside of time. To be sure, this very being set all the frameworks in place that make it possible for us to understand that there exists such an entity as time. Moreover, this being is also the creator of space. As with time, he set all the frameworks in place that make it possible for us to understand that there exists such an entity as space. Within the notion of space and time, there is also the question of matter and energy. It is held, within the circles of Christian theology, that God is the creator of matter as well as the source of energy that now runs the universe, or at least enables the universe to operate as it does.

Scientists like Richard Dawkins call this view into question, contending that seeing God as the cause of the universe is not an explanation at all, since this leaves us open to the question, "Who then created God?" Many serious theists believe that Dawkins' answer is meaningless if he uses God in the sense that theists use them. This is because theists understand God as an uncreated and uncaused being. It therefore makes no sense to ask, "Who caused an Uncaused Being?" or "Who created an Uncreated Being." One might well ask who moved the immovable object. If the object was moved, then it was no longer immovable. In other words, the terms destroy themselves conceptually before any meaning can be conveyed. Similarly, Dawkins' question destroys itself before it takes off the ground, hence it is nonsensical.

Philosophy aside, we must ask how it is that heaven will answer our questions of origin. First, it appears that once we see God face to face in heaven, we will discover almost immediately, that he is the one responsible for holding the universe together. More so, we will also discover that his power, which holds the universe together, is the very power that brought it into being in the first place; for we will see how the entire created order bows to his Lordship in ways that we could never have imagined. The universe may not strike us as conscious, but it will listen to the voice of the one who created it, and it will obey. We will discover why the storms obeyed Christ when he commanded them to be still. We will discover that he created nature, and that when nature comes face to face with the commands of its creator, it has to obey.

That God brought everything into existence, then, is an answer to a question that many unbelievers have asked, an answer that they have also rejected. It is also an answer that will shock them; for they will discover that what they rejected as a religious view turned out to be plausible over and above the view they believed was more academic.

Heaven, therefore, will decisively answer questions about our origin with triumphant finality. The question will be settled in a way never anticipated by philosophers, scientists and thinkers of other fields. Some speculation here might be in order. For example, perhaps God will somehow walk us through the process of how he set the foundations of the universe in place. Perhaps he will be more than happy to discuss with us how he miraculously brought about the creation of human beings. I suspect, however, that what we will see of God at that time will be so spectacular that we will need no explanation as to how God brought us into existence. Perhaps we will see him and wonder how a being with so much power could not have brought anything into existence. All this is speculation, though. At any rate, the point I am making is this: true answers about our origin will be available after the final page of the history of the universe is written. Let me now move to the question of meaning.

B. Heaven's Answer to the Question of Meaning

"What is the meaning of life?" is a question that reflective human beings ask. Non-religious thinkers maintain that there really is no overarching meaning to the universe that we live in. The only meaning available to such a universe is the one we give it. Of course many Christian thinkers, notably William L. Craig, find this view very problematic. For one, it is highly relativistic. Anybody can simply formulate his or her own view of meaning that could quite conceivably clash with another person's view, perhaps even violate another person's conception of meaning. Moreover, if there truly is no meaning in the universe, then we cannot find such meaning anywhere in the universe. Neither can we give meaning to such a universe precisely because we are part of the universe that lacks such meaning. To believe that we can smuggle meaning into an otherwise meaningless universe is intellectually self-stultifying.

However, I doubt that you, the reader, are interested in such hair-splitting arguments concerning the meaning of the universe. Perhaps what you are concerned about is to know why you are here. In other words, what goals or purposes are you supposed to fulfill in life? Is there some cosmic fabric, a plan of sorts, of which you are a part, such that if you fail to play your role, you will face some unpleasant consequences? Is there an overarching purpose in the universe such that if you fulfill it in your present life you will experience a life of ultimate satisfaction in the end?

In a sense, there is. The sense in which such a plan exists is not one that appears hidden from sight. It is one that has been so clearly explicated in Scripture. As noted in previous sections of this book, one of the reasons we were created by God is so that we might freely choose to love him and enjoy an eternal relationship of joy and happiness with him in heaven. For now, our hearts seem to long for just such a relationship. Augustine reminded us, for example, that our hearts are restless until they find rest in God. When our souls set eyes on their creator, they will at once realize that eternal union with God is what they were meant for.

When we see this as formulating a major aspect of the goal and purpose of our lives, living through this earthly life will perhaps be more bearable than it currently is. Again, as noted, we feel that something seems to be terribly wrong with the universe we live in, though in many ways, it is a habitable place. However, when we know that this is not the end of the story, that a better life of enjoyment with God is coming, we will find our lives here on earth a whole lot more meaningful.

Let us now consider the alternative view, one that claims that life is meaningless. We have already seen the self-defeating nature of this view. Let us assume, for one moment, that there is no purpose to life, that we are mere products of time, matter and chance reactions in a meaningless universe. On this view, we become the sort of product that William L. Craig calls "a cosmological miscarriage." A person laying claim to such a view does not have much hope for living.

The person in question must go down in life quite dejected and forlorn, for there seems to be no reason to persevere through, say, a terminal illness like cancer or through the heart-rending experience of watching a loved one languish to death through some kind of tragic suffering. The absence of meaning in pain is a terrible tragedy indeed. Not only can one not ask what the meaning of that pain is, for there is none; in addition, one cannot have any motivation to fight or persevere through a battle of this sort when one is already fully aware of the tragic outcome of utter defeat. Existentially, therefore, there seems to be no reason to subscribe to such a view.

The view of Scripture is more attractive. One feels motivated to live through one's illness, knowing that this is not the end of the story; that God will make things right in the final analysis; and that in the end suffering will be eliminated and good will triumph over evil. More so, one is assured that the end is coming with the promise of having the cravings of the human soul completely fulfilled through its re-union with the One who designed it for just this very purpose. It is for this reason that the Christian finds solace in these very powerful words from Romans 8:37 – 39:

> No, in all these things we are more than conquerors through him who loved us. For I am convinced that neither death nor life, neither angels nor demons, neither the present nor the future, nor any powers, neither height nor depth, nor anything else in all creation, will be able to separate us from the love of God that is in Christ Jesus our Lord.

What is the meaning of life, then, for the Christian? Part of the answer to the question is the anticipation of enjoying eternal life of happiness with God in heaven when the soul re-unites with God in knowledge of him and eternal relationship with him. I believe that when we get to heaven, our souls will be "at rest" (in the Augustinian sense) knowing that they will have reached the goal for which they were made.

I must quickly clarify what I mean by this re-union. It is not the kind of re-union adumbrated by Eastern Pantheistic Monism in which the soul loses its individual nature as when, for example, a drop of water loses its individual nature when it unites with a larger body of water. This re-union is the kind of re-union we experience when friends or family have been separated for some time, only to meet again at a later stage in life. I still insist, however, that this re-union will be more intimate than anything we could ever imagine, though quite frankly, I have no way of demonstrating this. We can only wait until that day to see exactly how it will happen. I now move to heaven's answer to the question of morality.

C. Heaven's Answer to the Question of Morality

What does it mean to be moral? Where does morality come from? Does it come from God? Or does it come from another source besides God? Is there a standard of morality out there that we all must plug into in order to determine whether we are living the good life? In other words, is there a set of rules out there that determine for us what right living entails, specifying conditions that must be fulfilled in order for a given course of action to be judged "the right thing to do"? Or is it the case that each person decides for himself what the right thing to do really is?

Quite interestingly, it is becoming increasingly popular to contend that there are no sets of rules above our own personal and individual rules. Each human being, the trend goes, must form his or her own set of rules and standards by which to conduct his or her life. In other words, an individual is free to prescribe his or her rules for him- or herself. Nevertheless, that individual should not make those rules morally binding on other people. This view is called moral relativism. It is the kind of view that dominates our culture today.

However, it is usually quite fascinating how moral relativism is itself practically unlivable. For example, the principle upon which moral relativism is based is a principle that the moral relativist believes applies to all people. The moral relativist therefore makes it a rule for all people that no one should apply his or her own personal rules to all people. In other words, no one should force his or her own personal rules on all people. Notice that the claim of moral relativism forbids the very claim it endorses! They are applying on all people the very rule that "no one should force his or her own personal rules on all people." Perhaps this is why moral relativists find themselves upholding their view in theory, but abandoning it in practice.

This issue has been dealt with at length in ethical philosophy, and any attempts to deal with it here will perhaps take us off course. I believe, however, that my brief take on moral relativism above is sufficient, at least initially, to expose the difficulties attending that view. Let me now turn to the other view, namely, that there exists a set of rules or standard, a set properly considered absolute, to which we must conform, such that we would be judged immoral if we fail to conform to that standard. This seems to be the only viable alternative, and it is a view philosophers call moral objectivism.

Moral objectivism holds that an absolute set of rules really and truly exists, and it is morally binding on all people irrespective of race, color or ethnic background. The big question here is just what this objective set of rules is. This then takes us back to the very first series of questions at the beginning of this section. If there exists a set of rules or some given standard to which we must conform, where does it come from?

Plato believed that morality comes from human reason, and that if we followed the principles of human reason, it will enable us to know The Absolute Good, which he called The Good Itself. In his Allegory of the Cave as well as his doctrine of the Divided Line, Plato comes extremely close to claiming that this Good Itself is identical with God. Just the same, that is as far as he goes.

Aristotle, Plato's student, rejected Plato's claim that the Good Itself is the highest good. He felt that this view of the good was way beyond our cognitive faculties, and was quite impractical in helping us live moral lives. So, whereas agreeing with Plato that morality comes from reason, he felt that the highest good, attainable by reason, is happiness. He felt that happiness is the highest good for three reasons: it is desirable for its own sake; it is not desirable for the sake of another; and everything else is desirable for its sake. Aristotle would therefore argue that when we think about it, all human beings desire to be happy. Happiness seems to be the goal of every human being. Hence happiness must be the highest good.

Much later, Epicurus felt that the highest good is a state of freedom from pain in the body and disturbance in the soul. He felt that a given course of action is good if pleasurable and bad if painful. Hence in his view, morality comes from pleasure. He noted, however, that sometimes we will need to avoid instances of pleasure that have long-term painful consequences. At other times we could be required to embrace instances of pain that have long-term pleasurable consequences.

The Stoic Epictetus, on the other hand, felt that morality comes from the will, and that self-discipline was the highest good. In his view, one was or is moral if one used or uses the will to control inner passions and emotions in a way that demonstrated self-discipline. Epictetus believed that a moral person was not the kind of person vulnerable to his or her inner emotions.

These four thinkers represented a majority of the ancient thinkers on what it means to be moral. Their influence was considerably great – enough to have modern philosophers embrace some of them. For example, utilitarianism, the view that we should strive to promote the greatest happiness for the greatest number of people, can be traced back to Epicurus. Modern day virtue ethicists, who emphasize inner character as a way of determining whether a person is moral or not, can be traced back to Plato and Aristotle.

Not all modern thinkers embraced the ancients wholesale. David Hume, for example, maintained that morality comes from feeling, which he variously termed 'sentiment' or 'taste.' But this feeling, according to David Hume, is a sense that the Divine Will implanted in the human person. So for Hume, there is a sense in which morality comes from God.[56] This should strike us as strange, in light of Hume's hostility to Christianity.

---

56   See David Hume's *An Enquiry Concerning the Principles of Morals,* ed. J. B. Schneewind (Indianapolis: Hackett, 1983), p. 87. There Hume writes: "The standard of the other [taste], arising from the internal frame and constitution of animals, is ultimately derived from the Supreme Will, which bestowed in each being its peculiar nature, and arranged the several classes and orders of existence."

While embracing the view that morality comes from reason, Immanuel Kant rejected the Aristotelian claim that the aim of reason is to produce happiness. For Kant, instinct does a better job than reason at producing happiness. Kant proposed, instead, that the goal of reason is to produce a morally good person. A morally good person is one who does the right thing specifically because that very act is the right thing to do even if one is tempted to do otherwise.

This brief survey is by no means exhaustive. I have omitted other important thinkers on this aspect, like Karl Marx and Friedrich Nietzsche, for example. Just the same, the survey serves to show that the debate on the source of morality indeed has a long and distinguished career. There seems to be no disagreements with regards to whether or not we should be moral. We all seem to agree on that. The bone of contention can be located on the source of morality, and for that matter, what the highest good entails. The answer to the question of what it means to be moral and of where morality comes from seems to be very elusive. Different philosophers have formulated different answers, with a number of latter philosophers refuting former philosophers.

Notice what I alluded to in the last paragraph above. There seems to be little or no disagreements as to whether or not we should be moral. This seems to be the key to helping us determine where morality comes from. We all agree that we should be moral. This implies that we are aware that there is a way in which we ought to behave. If indeed we are aware of this, it also implies that we must believe there exists a law "out there" that tells us how we should behave. If such a law exists, our next step is to ask where it came from. It certainly did not come from an unconscious source. This law must have come from a conscious source outside ourselves. This conscious source must have comprehensive knowledge of the human condition in order to prescribe for human beings how they should behave in different situations. It would appear that God is the best candidate for this conscious source.

I therefore think that Augustine and Aquinas were both essentially correct when they variously contended that morality comes from God. Augustine believed that God is the source of morality, and that the highest good is eternal life in heaven. Aquinas believed that reason is the source of morality, but this reason is given to us by Divine Reason, or God, for that matter. He believed that the highest good is the contemplation of God. In that sense, Aquinas not only reflected the Aristotelian view; he also seemed to give it a Christian bent.

Augustine's and Aquinas' views are consistent with Scripture. Scripture maintains that morality comes from God. In fact it would be correct to think of both the Old and New Testaments as a promulgation of God's law to human beings. Throughout Scripture we read of how God interacts with his people, and how he expects them to live. His call to holiness placed upon all his sentient beings is a case in point. It would be safe to say that this expectation, and these frequent calls to holiness, are made on the supposition that God has laws that must be obeyed. Further, they are made on the supposition that God is the source of these laws.

Consider this. If God is sovereign, he must be in control of everything. If he is in control of everything, then everything he controls must be subject to his sovereign power. If this is the case, we must conclude that God is the source of laws that govern our universe. Moreover, if he is the source of laws that govern the universe, it follows that the universe as we know it will come to an end only by God's sovereign declaration. Suppose then that God is in control of everything in this way, it has to follow that when he brings this current universe to an end in order to usher in the New Heaven and the New Earth, what will immediately be impressed upon us will be his authority, or put differently, his power to enforce his laws. We will be immediately aware that God is the guardian of the laws of which we were aware when we all agreed that there exists a set of laws out there.

Hence, in spite of the various ethical theories adopted by different thinkers and philosophers, heaven will reveal to us that the moral law which we all agree exists was a law put in place by God. It seems reasonable to suppose, further, that God will judge the world based on their conformity to this law. The question of judgment presupposes that God put his laws in place, and human beings will be called to answer for their conformity or non-conformity to such laws. It will not be pretty.

However, believers in Christ have been promised an advocate and mediator, namely, Jesus Christ, who will come to their defense when the time comes. Those who have accepted Christ as Lord and Savior need not be worried that they will miss the wonderful opportunity to spend eternal life of happiness in full enjoyment of their relationship with Christ. This does not imply that their lives ought to be lived carelessly. In fact, it is out of this state of moral carelessness that they have been called, and have been given the grace to live holy and righteous lives in conformity with God's moral laws. Heaven, more than any other place, will impress upon us the seriousness with which God required us to live our lives in obedience to those laws. I now turn to the question of identity.

D. Heaven's Answer to the Question of Identity

One of the strangest questions we have ever asked ourselves is that of who we are. What is it that makes us who we are? How is it that we are who we are rather than anything else? These questions sound rather silly on face value. Believe it or not, theologians, and more so, philosophers, have struggled with finding answers to these questions for centuries.

Ever since the arrival of Darwinian evolution, naturalists[57] are beginning to conclude that as human beings we have no special place or standing above other living species. We are as much a conglomeration of atoms and molecules as those species, and our thought processes are essentially a process of chemical firings in our brain. In other words, we are essentially material beings with no supernatural or immaterial entities, called souls, forming a part of our overall structure.

Of course, as noted in many different texts, there are serious problems with this view, at least from a Christian perspective. One

---

57 Roughly speaking, naturalists are people who believe that nature is all there is, and that supernatural entities like God, angels, souls and spirits do not exist.

such problem can be captured as follows. If our thoughts are merely the firing of chemicals in our brain, then we have no option but to think the way we do think, and as a consequence, to behave the way we do behave. If that is the case, it follows that people who do wrong have no option but to do wrong. Thus murderers, thieves, fornicators and adulterers cannot help being who they are. This would further mean that such people cannot be blamed for behaving the way they do; for their behavior corresponds to their ways of thinking, ways determined by the chemical firings of their brain.

On the contrary, we do believe that people ought to be held responsible for their actions. Murderers, thieves, liars, adulterers and rapists, we maintain, should be held accountable for their actions – actions which we believe are wrong. If so, we must also believe that such people behave the way they do, not because they could not have behaved otherwise, but because they exercised their own free will and chose the course of actions they now find themselves following. If we accept this view, we must reject the claim that human thought and reason is the result of chemical procedures or firings of chemical stimuli in the brain. Human thought seems to be quite independent of such procedures in many ways.

This is not the only difficulty we have with this materialistic account of the human person. If human thought is indeed conditioned or determined in the way described by the evolutionary agenda, we are faced with the question of trusting our rational faculties. If it is true that the human person is a conglomeration of atoms and molecules, then our thoughts must essentially arise from just those atoms and molecules. Those atoms and molecules are essentially non-rational, while our thoughts are supposed to be rational. Following C. S. Lewis we ask: can we really trust our rational faculties if they are based on non-rational foundations? This sounds seriously flawed.

It would therefore appear that strict atheistic Darwinian evolution fails to give us a full account of who we are. What it leaves us with is a description of a robotic species quite foreign to what we know as human beings. We must therefore begin to look for a description of who we are from a more plausible source.

Notice that the evolutionary account was formulated as a rejection of the Biblical account, which categorically states that humans have been made in the image of God. The Biblical account affirms that human beings have a very distinct aspect in them that gives them their identity. They have been created as people who think, relate and communicate. Their mental processes are not based on non-rational foundations. They are based on Divine Reason, the source of all thinking. This seems to best account for human reason than the evolutionary model.

The human being, then, according to the Biblical model, is created in the image of God. Images are reflections of the original. Hence, there is a sense in which human beings are a reflection of God, so to speak. If that is the case, it must follow that humans ought to trace their identity back to God. Hence, the answer to the question of who we are must include this sense of identity with God.

If we must trace our source or sense of identity back to God, it means that when we finally meet with God face to face in heaven, that sense of belonging will be most fully realized and understood for what it is. The human soul will at once recognize and feel that it was made for just this very purpose of identifying itself with God, that is, in the sense of belonging to the one who made it with infinite love.

Heaven will therefore reveal to us our full identity. It will fully reveal to us the idea of what it means to be created in the image of God. It will become clear to us not only how precious we have always been to God, but how ecstatic he has been about us, the crown of his creation. The experience will perhaps be more moving than the joy parents have when their long lost child finally returns home to the warm embrace of their parents. Not only shall we, as God's children, delight in "landing in the arms of our heavenly father" so to speak, but God himself will delight in holding us close to himself as his very own. This will be the joy of discovering who we are and whose we are.

E. Heaven's Answer to the Question of Destiny

My Grandfather died when I was about five years old. That was the first time I ever saw a dead body – the body of a person I knew. Watching my father wailing uncontrollably at the passing of his own father moved me beyond description. I immediately put myself in my father's shoes. His father had just died in the bedroom after a long fight with diabetes, and some other abdominal complications I could never understand. I imagined how I would have felt had my father died. It troubled me deeply that my father was grieving in this way. He held my hand, pacing up and down the living room of his father's house, sobbing loudly and recounting the years he had spent with his father. It was one of the most painful things for me to watch in my pre-teen years. I grieved in my own way, though quite frankly, I do not remember how. I remember crying. I also remember feeling a sense of hopelessness, in light of the fact that my father, who was my hero then, was feeling hopeless as well.

It was then that I began to wonder about the whole question of destiny. Of course I never knew about the word itself. I did wonder, though, whether this was all there is to life. I wondered whether death was the final stage of our lives followed by the complete extinction of the individual's consciousness. I knew my grandfather was a Christian, perhaps one of the most respected Christians in our village. However, I had not formulated a personal eschatology. I was too young to formulate one.

I do recollect speaking with some of my cousins shortly thereafter concerning what happens when and after we die. In their own theology of destiny, they told me that my grandfather had gone to heaven. That did not make sense to me. How could he go to heaven when his body was clearly there, lying motionless? So I prodded further. Their response, now that I think about it, was less than satisfactory, but it somehow worked for me then. However, upon thinking about it much, much later, it sounded really hilarious. They told me that God came down and took my grandfather's soul to heaven. The reason this did not make sense to me is this. In my native language, the word for soul is really the same word for liver. It is also the same word for "essence." I was too young to understand the notion of "essence." So I immediately assumed that, as per my cousins' explanation, God came and took my grandfather's liver to heaven. Why would God choose my grandfather's liver, out of the rest of his body, to take with him to heaven? Not being able to find an answer to that question, I decided to abandon the whole project of thinking about life after death.

Much later, when I was in a primary boarding school, I heard for the first time, and in full detail, about the promise of Christ's return. The Sunday school teacher seemed well versed in her theology to explain to us about the Second Coming of Christ. The explanation shook me to the core. I knew I had to do something about it. I had to be prepared for Christ's coming. Unfortunately for me, I did not know what I needed to do. When I was close to completing my final year of primary education, I heard the Gospel for the first time proclaimed in a clear way. I made a commitment to follow Christ as my Lord and Savior, but I must confess I was not sure of what I was doing. Just the same, in my first year of high school education, a friend of mine explained the Gospel to me in a clearer way, and I became a Christian. Still, I lacked the requisite discipleship that would establish my faith in Christ. My grounding in the faith came about through the discipleship of a brother by the name of Scott Herbert, who finally prayed with me and helped counsel me into the possibility of joining full time ministry.

I draw attention to my testimony here for a simple reason. I was very concerned about human destiny. Where are we going? More specifically, where was I going? Would my life end in death? Or would I live eternally? If I lived eternally, where would I spend it? Would I spend it in eternal damnation or would I spend it in eternal joy with the Triune God?

My friend, Scott Herbert, from Oregon, helped establish this for me. He reminded me that only in Christianity can we be assured of where we are going; for only in Christianity are we reminded that those who believe in the name of the Son of God have eternal life, and that God sent his only begotten Son and that whoever believes in him will not perish but have eternal life.

Scott Herbert narrated a conversation he had with a Muslim friend of his. He asked the Muslim whether there was any assurance of salvation in Islam. Of course the individual said he had none. Herbert then pointed out that he would rather follow a system of belief that offered him the assurance of salvation than subscribe to one bereft of one. This assurance, Herbert correctly observed, is found in Christianity. That settled it for me. It went a long way in beginning to ground me in the faith. It was after this form of assurance that I began to pursue the possibility of joining the Christian ministry as a full time pastor.

When I consider the different options offered concerning the question of destiny, I find the Christian view unrivaled. It offers so much hope, and a promise of great joy in the final analysis. This life is not all there is to our existence. So much more has been offered by way of eternal life. The assurance that once we believe in Jesus, we can spend a life of eternal happiness in him is one that is simply second to none. It is an assurance of hope and destiny that no other system of faith can provide.

The question of destiny is important for the suffering believer. It reminds us that our pains and sufferings and tragedies are here only for a little while. For every individual, if each must suffer, such pain will be here, at most, for one hundred years. Following this brief period of human existence, there is a lifetime of eternal joy and holy bliss awaiting every believer in Jesus Christ. Nothing compares with it. It will be one joyous experience that, as earlier mentioned, no human person should miss. Once we set foot in that place, we will discover that this is where we were meant to be, for even though we will be seeing it for the first time, we will discover, immediately, that heaven truly is our destiny – our home.

VII. Heaven is a Place of Abundant Life

Now that we know that our questions about origin, morality, meaning, identity and destiny will be answered in heaven, along with other unanswered questions we might have here on earth, we are left believing that there is a lot more to heaven than simply escaping a life of eternal damnation and misery in hell. It will involve the soul's eternal re-union with its creator in a blessed relationship of pure, holy love and happiness. In other words, it will involve the soul's experience of the abundant life that Jesus promised to give to all his followers. Hence, in heaven, Christ's promise of being the giver of abundant life will be fully realized.

Several years ago a family friend died tragically in a swimming accident. David Gichuru[58] had travelled to California, from Wilmore, Kentucky, for a short vacation with his family. His intention was to return to Wilmore the following Monday after the vacation, and continue with his work as a chaplain at the University of Kentucky Hospital. On the first day of their vacation, which was a Friday, the Gichuru family and the family that hosted them both went out to the beach for a day of fun in the west coast ocean water, swimming and watching their young ones swim as well. Shortly thereafter, they were warned that a riptide was approaching. The approach of this riptide must have caught David's sons unprepared. In the process of

---

58   This story is published here with the consent of Grace Gichuru, David's sur-
     viving widow.

rescuing his sons from the riptide, somehow David drowned. When he was finally pulled out of the water and rushed to hospital, David was gone.

I was in Wilmore then, and had spoken with David briefly over the phone earlier that day. To hear, within a span of five hours, that David was gone, felt like the worst nightmare anyone could have. For one, David had just completed his Masters Degree at Asbury Seminary, and was preparing to return to Kenya for ministry. His future was promising. He was excited about returning to his home country. We shared his excitement with him. Being next door neighbors, we spent many evenings of dinner together, and many mornings at breakfast. We therefore felt as if the most precious jewel had been snatched from us so unexpectedly.

David was a jewel of sorts at Asbury Seminary. Never mind that he was an international student. He was known as a true servant of the people. He helped new students settle in their new homes in Wilmore. He would cancel or postpone his pastime to help new arrivals unload their belongings from their trucks. If anyone needed to replace a washing machine or a dryer, David was the man for the job. If a student needed beddings, or new pieces of furniture, David was the man to do it. He did it with such grace and selflessness that touched the community of students and faculty at Asbury Seminary. His positive impact on the community was such that when it was David's time to move to a different apartment, he had too many people showing up to help.

Moreover, when David transitioned from Asbury Seminary to the University of Kentucky to become one of the hospital chaplains there, his influence as a servant spread quickly. His smile was contagious. His playfulness was something he never left behind. The amazing thing about David was the fact that he was respectfully fearless. On a certain occasion, he did not shy away from correcting the president of the seminary when he felt the seminary did not handle a certain issue correctly. He carried his fearlessness wherever he went. Nothing seemed to intimidate him. When I defended my dissertation, he came to support me, and sat in the room throughout the defense. David made it no secret to my dissertation panel, which was largely composed of unbelievers, that he was a chaplain and a Christian for that matter. He was cheerful throughout the process – a process that would have been emotionally overwhelming had David not been there.

I draw attention to David's story for one specific reason: he lived his life abundantly. His wife Grace, and sons, Amos and Jesse, are people that David lived for. He lived abundantly for them. He also lived abundantly for God. Due to the abundant life he found in Christ, he was able to live that life and enrich people's lives with his Christ-likeness. I strongly believed that I was David's best friend, and vice-versa. However, I was wrong. David was everyone's best friend – at least this was the case with the ones that knew him like we did.

David was excited about life. He was excited about what the Lord had in store for him. He lived his life to the fullest. He looked for opportunities to make people happier and more comfortable specifically because he was happy and comfortable. He was generous with his money. Rumor has it that he gave so much of it away and saved very little for his own personal needs. Even with this kind of generosity, David provided for his family just as responsibly as any father would do. He loved his family more than anything else in the world. He loved his Lord Jesus Christ above everything else, and he was willing to do anything he believed the Lord was leading him to do.

When David died, people wondered why God took him away so soon. He was just beginning to settle and to enjoy his life with his family. We may never be able to answer this question this side of heaven. One thing we immediately discover from David's example is the illustration of abundant life that the memory of his earthly life brings to our attention. Suppose everyone was like David. The world would be a much better place to live in. There would be fewer sorrows, more happiness and greater comfort in such a world. Whereas such a world seems beyond reach here on earth, it is well within reach in our eternal home. More accurately, when we envision heaven, we are looking at a world where kindness, comfort, happiness, and all these gifts, will not be for a season, as was the case with David's life. We will enjoy them forever. They will be there to stay; for they will be emanating from God himself. This reminds us of the promise that God shall wipe away all our tears, for the old order of things will have passed away.

As we look at our lives today, they are anything but abundant. The theme of suffering, which we have encountered quite at length in this book, denies us the freedom to enjoy our lives. We must also remember, though, that pain has some benefits. For example, in order to be healthy, we must experience the pain of exercise. Without pain, patience and perseverance (which we believe are virtues) would not be necessary. Consider, for example, that the sensation of pain is what makes us release our grip on a hot surface. In that case, it is good that we have it. Sometimes pain is information, communicating to us that something, out of which the pain is emerging, is seriously wrong and needs fixing.

Arguing for this benefit of pain, Phillip Yancey wrote a book entitled *Pain: The Gift Nobody Wants*. One of his major contentions throughout that book is that a life without pain is definitely worse than a life with pain. If he is right (and I believe he is), there is a sense in which our flesh, blood and bones seem to benefit from the sensation of pain. Hence in this world, there is a sense in which life would not be abundant unless we had some pain in it. In other words, as long as we have flesh blood and bones, we will benefit, at some point in our lives, with the presence of pain than without it.

To illustrate this notion further, it is widely regarded by many ethicists, that people who live through moments of intense suffering come out more mature at the end of their suffering. This is amply shown, for example, by the analogy of materials used for building the finest pianos. It is understood that in order to build a good piano, the pieces of wood used for building it must come from trees that have withstood a lifetime of severe storms; for such trees will develop a sturdiness that would not be found among trees with shallow roots – roots that find nutrients readily available on the top soils.

Similarly, believers who fail to go through trying times (like tragedy and suffering) miss out on the importance of becoming more and more mature in their walk with the Lord. When times of trial finally come, they cannot hold out, and perhaps fall away. Therefore a person without such severe experiences of trial, pain and suffering, will perhaps be missing out on the benefit of becoming more and more mature in Christ. This helps, once again, to remind us that pain is perhaps not altogether bad. Perhaps it is not altogether undesirable. This is an uncomfortable but necessary benefit for us. That is why Yancey calls pain "a gift."

We must ask, though, whether we will need pain in heaven in the manner in which we "need" pain on earth. Of course, according to Scripture, there will be no more pain in heaven. Character building instances of pain, suffering and tragedy are instances that will have accomplished their purposes here on earth. If pain has the purpose of making us more mature, there is still the process of glorification which every believer will undergo. The notion of glorification is captured by the fact that believers, at this stage of their salvation, will be saved from the presence of sin. In other words, sin will be completely removed from their nature. Hence everything that keeps believers from attaining the spiritual maturity that they will need as they enter heaven will be removed. Hence in heaven believers will not need experiences of pain to make them more mature. They will already be mature by the removal of sin in their lives.

This serves to show that abundant life in heaven begins with our glorification. Our glorified bodies will experience lives richer and fuller than the lives we live in our current bodies. For one, our glorified bodies will no longer succumb to sicknesses and diseases, as we noted in an earlier chapter. They will also not be susceptible to pain. This is because the things that cause these instances of suffering will be removed from among us, and we will thus be free of them. The joy of this is nuanced further by the grand promise that pain and suffering will never afflict us again. This is at least one aspect of abundant life.

There is a second aspect of abundant life – the realization that our souls will be happily and forever nourished by the joy of the Lord. Some have called this eternal happiness. Others have called it eternal joy. Whatever one calls it, the one thing that will immediately strike us with great profundity is our discovery that human life here on earth is not only very short, but also severely limited, and that our new found life in heaven is infinitely richer and eternally joyful. We will discover that our earthly life is infinitely small compared to the magnitude of the abundance of life in heaven.

Consider some of the things we will experience there. We will experience eternal comfort. In other words, we will never be tormented by the reality of death any more. Death will no longer be a reality. This is the sort of victory over death that the Apostle Paul discussed in 1 Corinthians 15. A life without death is quite clearly a life of great abundance indeed!

Our souls will finally find relief from the deadly suffering and tragedies we will have faced here on earth. Goodbyes will be gone forever. Funerals will be gone forever. Burials will be gone forever. Death will be gone forever. All this is to say that we will no longer be plagued by these realities; for even though they are realities for us in the present, they will no longer be realities in the future. This is great comfort, and it is the kind of comfort that can be given only by our Lord Jesus Christ. We are promised that our tears shall all be wiped away, and our pain will be eliminated.

Not only shall we experience eternal comfort; we shall also experience eternal love. As relational beings, we long for love here on earth. Unfortunately, every kind of love we experience will come to an end in this life. The love we receive from our parents, our siblings and our friends comes to an end when they die. The love we receive from our spouses comes to an end when they die. Love, in a sense, fills our lives with some kind of meaning, though not the sort of ultimate meaning we seek when we try to discover what the overarching purpose of the universe is, including our place in it. That is why when relationships break, we feel considerable pain. This pain is at its peak when loved ones die.

It is gravely ironic that even in a wedding ceremony, which is supposed to be the happiest time of anyone's life, we are reminded of the saddest time of anyone's life by the clause that only death will separate the newlyweds. Perhaps that is why when a loved one dies we who are left behind feel so much pain. We feel pain, not only because, through death, a meaningful relationship has been broken, but also because death is itself a process that brings such finality to the love we received from the loved one now deceased.

Just the same, the promise of heaven is powerful. It is a promise that once we get to heaven, we will not only receive all the love we needed and longed for. We will receive it in abundant measures – we will receive it eternally. It will never come to an end. It will never come to us piece meal. It will never come with strings attached. It will come fully, abundantly and freely; for something like experiencing the full extent of God's love is the sort of thing entailed by abundant life. This will be an amazing and dramatic discovery.

We will discover that God's love, which we were receiving all the time on earth, is love that God has always been offering us without hesitation, without reservation and with great delight. We will discover that it is the same love expressed within the Triune God when, for example, two times God the Father said of God the Son: "This is my beloved Son, with whom I am well pleased." To be loved with the love of God will be more thrilling and more fulfilling than the sum total of the love we receive from our parents, friends and spouses. It will be love so unrivaled that we will be embarrassed for the simple reason that we did not reciprocate the same love to God.

Jesus' promise to us that he came to give us life, and to give it abundantly rings true of the promise of heaven. The words of the hymn *Amazing Grace* echo this very thought of abundant life in the following way:

> When we've been there ten thousand years
> Bright shining as the sun
> We've no less days to sing God's praise
> Than when we first begun!

Implicit in these words is the fact of a never ending life. We live in a world where everything must come to an end. Everything we do, irrespective of whether it involves sleep, school, eating, jogging, shopping or running, must all come to an end. This includes the pleasures we allow ourselves to enjoy – boating, a visit to the mall, to the stadium, or to the amusement park or a drink at a restaurant. These temporary things seem to be the sorts of things that define our lives. Moreover, other things that we hold dear to our lives will also come to an end just like the rest.

For example, our formal education comes to an end when we graduate. Our careers come to an end when we retire. With these achievements ending, as they eventually will, their corresponding certifications plummet in value, irrespective of whether they are associate degrees, doctoral degrees, or the sorts of awards and accolades we earn in life. We cannot take these to the grave with us, and no one will use them when we are gone. This is a grim reality, in light of the fact that most of these are considered lifetime achievements.

Nevertheless, there is one thing that need not come to an end for us, and that is our lives. Life is the one thing we can take with us to the grave, and still have beyond the grave. More specifically, once we have gone beyond the grave, we can still enjoy life to the fullest and to its greatest abundance. This is possible only when we make the right choices here on earth. I refer to the choice of surrendering both to the saving grace of our Lord Jesus Christ, and to his Lordship. This is a choice that God has given us the privilege of making.

The other possibility is that we can make the wrong choices, thereby gambling our lives away to eternal destruction. The unfortunate thing, however, about eternal destruction, is not that God is sending unbelievers there. It is a destiny the unbelievers choose for themselves. When they make a lifetime decision of desiring nothing to do with God, God has no option but to respect their choices and honor their request. That is what eternal damnation implies – a life in which God is completely out of the picture. It will not be pretty in any way. More specifically, it will be a life of extreme pain and suffering – for that is what a life that goes contrary to God's character entails. In other words, it is the full realization of a godless life that the unbeliever has throughout his life been insisting on leading.

By contrast, the promise of heaven is a life of abundance. The option has been placed before all people: either to choose eternal life with all its benefits, glories and promises of enjoying an eternal relationship with God, or to choose a life of endless destruction filled with misery, pain and meaninglessness. The surprising thing is that many are going for this second option with eyes wide open. The one who rejects this second option, and chooses the option of eternal life, will truly know what abundant life entails.

Of course it is possible for the skeptic to contend that the promise of heaven is in no way a guarantee of its existence. He or she might contend that such a promise is really based on wishful thinking that human beings have placed on themselves. This is because, having discovered that earthly life is unlivable in many ways, they develop a longing for the possibility that it could have been different, filled with joy, happiness, comfort, pleasure and with little or no pain at all. Hence the person skeptical of what he or she thinks is the "so-called promise of heaven" would contend that one ought to live one's life here to the fullest rather than hope for something human beings have no clue about.

It is not my intention to fully answer the skeptic here. I believe such objections have been amply met in other pieces of literature. I refer here to Jerry Walls' philosophical work entitled *Heaven: The Logic of Eternal Joy*. However, it would perhaps be helpful to consider several reasons, outside the Bible, why Christian believers are not mistaken, or even deluded into thinking that a place called heaven exists, a place where our eternal and joyous relationship with the Lord will finally be experienced by those of us who surrender to his bidding.

One such argument[59] was provided by the medieval philosopher, Thomas Aquinas. Aquinas contended that God created human beings for an ultimate purpose. This purpose, in Aquinas' view, is happiness. This is a purpose that God will not fail to achieve. Noting that this state of happiness will definitely not be achieved in this life, and since God could not have created us in vain, we

---

59 For a summary of Aquinas' arguments, see *Reason and Religious Belief* 4th edition, edited by Michael Peterson (New York: Oxford University Press, 2009) p. 233 - 234

will somehow achieve this happiness in another life, and this quite logically requires that our lives continue even after we die.

The sort of happiness that Aquinas has in mind here, however, is the kind that we get when we fulfill the purpose for which we are made – which in Aquinas view is the contemplation of God. In this life, Aquinas would say, we cannot fully contemplate God. Just the same, we will fully contemplate him in life after death. Of course many skeptical philosophers will question some of Aquinas' presuppositions, including his contention that God's creation would be compromised if we fail to achieve our ultimate end. We must always remember, though, that God has created us with free choice. Hence if we consciously choose to follow a life-path that fails to meet this goal, God need not be the one to blame; rather, we are.

Another reason some philosophers have concerning belief in life after death is the one found in the moral argument. It was originally formulated by Immanuel Kant.[60] The argument recognizes that our existence as human beings is not sufficient to achieve the moral ideal. Neither is it sufficient to provide an adequate standard on which to recommend choosing the good rather than choosing evil. However, the moral law seems to tell us that we must strive to achieve the highest good. If we cannot attain this highest good, we cannot be commanded to achieve it. The reality, however, is that this highest good cannot be achieved in this life. Therefore, if we are to be obligated to live under the moral law, we must somehow be able to live past death – at least to the point at which we can become holy.

One will see that these are arguments based on reason without experience; hence one will feel that if we had arguments based both on reason and experience we would formulate a more cogent package. The most popular argument for believing in life after death is what many would call near death experiences. These are experiences of individuals who almost died or who were declared dead and then resuscitated.

A general account of near death experiences can be captured as follows. Many individuals, lying at the point of death in hospital,

---

60 See a summary of Kant's argument from Peterson's *Reason and Religious Belief,* p. 234

testified that they heard their nurses and doctors pronouncing them dying, or dead. Following the pronouncements, they find themselves 'outside' their body, and perceiving their immediate environment from a different view. What they perceived, for example, included their health-care personnel desperately trying to resuscitate their body. They also discovered that they possessed a new body, sometimes described as an amorphous cloud or a spiritual body, but somehow shaped like their physical body. They then saw themselves passing through a dark place, usually described as a tunnel, until they come to a different realm, where they seemed to meet other persons, known or unknown to them, some of whom they recognized, even though disembodied, and with whom they communicated in a way reminiscent of telepathy. More interestingly, they spoke of encountering a being of light, exuding love and compassion. The being seemed to help them recall and evaluate their past. In spite of their desire to stay and enjoy their wonderful experience, some of them still wanted, or were commanded to return to their physical bodies.[61]

Many have expressed doubt concerning these experiences. Some skeptics, for example, believe that the experiences are really hallucinations brought about by physiological conditions in the body. Others have argued that non-believers and adherents of other religious traditions seem to have experiences similar to those of believers. Hence, they conclude, this experience cannot be used to confirm biblical doctrine of the afterlife. Quite interestingly, though, descriptions of immediate circumstances surrounding the physical bodies given by persons with near death experiences demonstrate amazing accuracy.

Irrespective of what one might say concerning these experiences, let me draw attention to perhaps the most famous near death experience described by A. J. Ayer, an atheistic philosopher who not only debated Christians on the existence of God, but who also died an atheist. According to Ayer, his heart had stopped for four minutes. He describes his experience as follows: "I was surrounded by a red light, exceedingly bright, and also very painful, even when

---

61   Peterson, p. 231

I turned away from it. I was aware that this light was responsible for the government of the universe."[62]

Several years back, I taught a class on "death and dying" at the University of Kentucky. When we approached the topic of near death experiences, I had them read this account by Ayer. One student came to me immediately after class and observed, at once, that Ayer's experience seems not only consistent with Christian doctrine, but also solemnly reflective of a person who died and went to hell. If Ayer's experience is true (I find no reason to think it untrue), he must have been exposed to the ultimate consequences of unbelief, hence confirming what the Bible has been teaching all along about those who die without making a decision.

Many more stories exist about those who were declared dead and found themselves in an environment they understood either as heaven, or somehow consistent with the Christian doctrine of heaven. Jerry Walls gives a sufficient demonstration of such cases in his book.

The most famous account of life after death, of course, is the death and resurrection of Jesus Christ. The death and resurrection of Christ, according to the Bible, is the basis for belief in life after death and enjoyment of heaven for Christians submitting to the Lordship of Jesus Christ. According to the Apostle Paul, if Jesus was not raised from the dead, then we are to be the most pitied of all people. Following Michael Peterson and his cohorts, the argument can be restated as follows: If Christ was raised from the dead, we will be raised from the dead. Christ was indeed raised from the dead. Therefore, we will be raised from the dead.[63]

As the authors of *Reason and Religious Belief* note, in order to accept this argument from the resurrection as true, one must also be willing to accept other claims of Christianity, including the contention that God exists and that he has revealed himself to his creation, and most notably, to human beings created in his image.

---

62 A. J. Ayer, "What I Saw When I Was Dead," first printed in *Spectator*, July 16 1968, subsequently reprinted in *The Philosophy of A. J. Ayer*, ed. L. E. Hahn (Open Court, 1992), p. 48

63 Peterson, p. 233

The orthodox Christian will have little difficulty accepting these claims. However, the skeptic will quite likely call all of them to question.

The point I want to press is this: Christians have every good reason to believe in the doctrine of eternal life in heaven. No other system of belief can offer this hope in the way Christianity does. Most systems of belief focus their attention on this world and forget about the next world. Others seem to focus their attention on the next world and forget about this world. A balanced Christian view, however, seems to focus its attention both on this world and the next world, maintaining that the choices we make in this world will ultimately affect where we spend eternity in the next.

One could choose a life of eternal misery and ruin by rejecting Christ as Lord and Savior. Alternatively, one could have the living hope of eternal life in Christ by accepting Christ. As already noted, this will be the fulfillment of the promise of eternal life. It is a life of endless joy, love and deep fulfillment shared between redeemed saints of God and the Triune God himself. This is something that we ought not to pass up, as human beings created in the image of God. Rather, we should embrace it wholeheartedly, knowing that life immeasurable awaits us on the other side.

VIII. Conclusion

Having come this far, we must now pause to ask ourselves the following question: what are the implications of heaven for our earthly lives here below? In other words, knowing that heaven is our final and eternal destination, how should we then live? Should we live as people completely detached from earth's experiences, or should we be more involved in living life to the fullest here below? Should we sit back and do nothing, waiting for the end of the world to come, or should we find meaningful ways of living our earthly lives? I contend that it is precisely the hope of heaven that enables us to live meaningful lives on earth. It is precisely because of this hope that we aim and strive to improve the quality of our lives as well as those of others. It is precisely because of this hope that we must preach the gospel both in word and deed. We preach the word in the former way because many today need to know that a life of comfort and joy awaits them on the other side of death if they pledge allegiance to Jesus Christ in full surrender to him as Lord and Savior of their lives. We also preach the word in the latter way with actions that give a relatively minute foretaste of heaven to those with no more reason for living, to those believing that no more comfort is available for whatever they think is left of their lives.

Allow me to draw from two similar experiences I had, when I was in Bible school, and when I was in seminary. When I first joined Bible school, I knew it would take me four years to complete my degree in theology. When I tried to look at the implications of living in the college dormitory for four years, I was overwhelmed by the very thought itself. I could not imagine how I could persevere through four years of biblical Greek, for example, and four years of studying theology. The assignments that I needed to complete were heavy, perhaps too heavy to be completed in four years. I began thinking that the professors, Christians though they seemed to be, were perhaps conspiring to make our Bible school experience as torturous as possible. Of course I was wrong about the professors.

We struggled through the semesters until the end of the year, during which the seniors began their graduation preparations. A banquet was held in their honor with the menu being nothing short of delicious. Top prizes were given to those that excelled in class. They had gone through their pain for the past four years, and had prevailed. Since I was a student choir director, I was asked to put together a small band that would play for the graduates as they marched towards their assigned places.

On the day of their graduation, families and friends gathered to witness their loved ones walk up the pavilion to receive their diplomas as their names were sequentially called. The applause, the cheering, the dancing and the high honor given to the graduates on that day was to stay in my memory for a long time to come. I could not help replaying the pomp and good cheer witnessed throughout the ceremony. The faculty members, who in my opinion were highly respectable (and still are to this day), were finally recognizing the academic efforts of the graduates. It all fell into place as I began looking forward to my own graduation. *So this is how my graduation will be!* The thought that I would one day receive the same honor and recognition stirred a yearning and a determination in my heart.

This was not the sort of honor that anyone of us considered prideful, or for that matter, sinful. It was not the sort of honor that I had set out to achieve earlier in my career (see page nine). This was the honor that was given in recognition of the fact that the students of the Bible had gone through rigorous training, difficult financial challenges, painful experiences (like losing loved ones), and they had come through considerably refined for ministry. I knew that challenges lay ahead of me in pursuing my theological training. The one I feared most was my suspicion that my father would probably not attend my graduation.

In spite of this, I promised myself that if God allowed me, I would stop at nothing in my training until I walked through the same pavilion victoriously with my diploma in hand. If this meant suffering through the academic rigors of biblical Greek, hermeneutics, homiletics or apologetics, I would be ready. If it meant suffering through the challenges of raising the finances required for the course, I would do my best to get the money. If it meant living through days of personal suffering, I would not allow it to take my eyes off the prize,

Halfway through college, my New Testament professor happened to use the Transfiguration of Jesus Christ as a lesson for all of us. Of course the Transfiguration was a lesson in itself. However, the professor used this very illustration to drive home the point that the Transfiguration of Jesus was analogous to witnessing his own graduation before he actually graduated. In other words, the transfiguration was a foretaste of Christ's own glorification which he would achieve after rising from the dead. We were reminded that this would happen only after Jesus had gone through the experience of suffering and dying for our sins.

Let me recollect the story for you. Jesus takes Peter, James and John with him up a high mountain. Once they reach the summit, Jesus' clothes suddenly become exceedingly bright, followed immediately by the appearance of Moses and Elijah, who begin talking to Christ. Notice the subject of their conversation: they begin talking to Christ about his imminent death. It would seem to be the case that seeing a glimpse of his glory in this way enabled him to endure and persevere through his crucifixion. Scripture confirms this when it writes: "And being found in appearance as a man, he humbled himself and became obedient to death – even death on a cross! Therefore *God exalted him to the highest place* and gave him the name that is above every name."[64]

This story, juxtaposed with my graduation experience, had a powerful impact in my life. As it turned out, the academic rigors

---

64 Philippians 2: 8, 9 [Emphasis mine]

were excruciating. I nearly dropped out due to lack of finances. My father died a year before my graduation. He was followed in death by my uncle, his brother. Twice I had to travel home by public means to bury both of them. It was difficult to watch my mother stand by my father's graveside as his casket was lowered into the grave. I had no idea that my training in theology would involve so much of life's severities. However, when I finally received my diploma, the applause I got was what one gets, not because of achieving so much, but because of having gone through so much in life and prevailing through it all by God's power.

The story does not end there. When I joined seminary in the United States, I was far removed from my home and my people. It was extremely difficult to be so far from home and family without making any regular contact with them by phone; for those were days when emails and cell phones were beginning to flood the market. However, when I witnessed the seniors graduating, I knew I wanted to have that experience as well. I felt ready to tackle the academic challenges placed before me, irrespective of the cultural differences I was forced to live through. However, having gone through what I went through in Bible school, I knew what walking up the graduation ramp entailed. It entailed a history of struggles, pain, sorrows, tears, suffering and death of loved ones.

As I completed my Bible school education, the graduation was not exactly everything I expected it to be. Friends and family came from different places to rejoice with me. They also knew what I had gone through, which made their rejoicing extremely meaningful for me. My graduation from seminary was just as meaningful. Just the same, I did not have as many friends or family to witness the experience. However, back home they understood the significance of this experience not just for me, but for them as well.

All this is to say that significant experiences of this sort, when anticipated somewhere in our future, help us to endure the struggles we face on this earth. We learn from Christ's experiences that his Transfiguration empowered him to face his experiences triumphantly. That is why, as Scripture reminds us, God exalted him to the highest place and gave him the highest and most powerful name.

I wish to suggest that the hope of heaven does the very same thing for us today. We are looking forward to inhabiting a dwelling place not made by human hands but by God himself. It will be a place where God himself shall wipe away all tears. He will do away with death, crying and pain. It will be a life forever filled with victory over suffering and evil. It will also be filled with great rejoicing – rejoicing in the full realization that this great wonderful life with our Blessed Redeemer Jesus Christ has now been placed before us to enjoy forever without end.

Knowing that this is where we are heading should give meaning to everything we do, irrespective of whether we are taking a road-trip to some intended destination, completing humanitarian projects, or walking to a stadium to watch a ballgame. The fact that we will enjoy our eternal destiny in heaven is no reason for us to suspend such activities, as long as, of course, they are not sinful. The flip side of the coin is also true: knowing that heaven is our final destiny should give meaning to the instances of suffering we face in our earthly lives. This is especially so in light of the promise that these sufferings are only temporary.

Perhaps we should learn from St. Francis of Assisi. As he was digging his garden, he was asked what he would do if he knew that Christ was coming the next day. The saint simply noted that he would finish digging his garden. The hope of Christ's return did not only give him meaning in doing what he was doing; it gave him meaning in doing it well.

When faced with the knowledge of Christ's return, many Christians get tempted to abandon accomplishing significant projects. I submit that those projects should be completed precisely because Christ is returning. Whether or not we complete the projects in question, we must remember that the question is not whether or not we have completed the projects; rather, it is about whether or not we have allowed the hope of heaven to make us live meaningful lives here below. Indeed, that seemed to be a major purpose of biblical prophecy, namely: to spur believers to live lives that would honor God here and now so that the gospel would be spread through the lives of believers in practical living. Hence, knowing that heaven is our destiny should give us a reason not only to read more and celebrate our earthly lives more; but also to worship the Lord more. It is both a "this-worldly" and an "other-worldly" celebration.

Before I bring this book to a close, one more thing should be said. All too often, heaven has been depicted as a place filled with dullness and boredom. In many ways it has been presented as a place where believers will sing old rusty hymns that seem to characterize dead churches today. Moreover, the argument goes, it will be a place completely lacking in excitement, luster, enjoyment, and all those attributes characteristic of a desirable life. If heaven is anything of this kind, the argument goes, no one really needs to hear anymore of it.

Several things need to be said about this contention. First, it is indeed unfortunate that some Christians have given an inaccurate view of heaven in their worship. Perhaps the churches are indeed dull and boring and the worship experience is itself something that no thinking person should look forward to. I well recall the words of an African New Testament scholar who reminded us of the seven words of a dying church: "we have always done it this way." According to him, churches that stick to this motto are those characterized by dullness and boredom of the sort described above.

However, as a second point, whereas the objection correctly notes that some churches are indeed as boring and dull as cemeteries, the objection itself is definitely based on an error. The fact of the matter is that no form of excitement exists here on earth whose functional substitute heaven will fail to provide in its purest and most infinite form. All forms of enjoyment and pleasure that we experience here on earth originated from God before some of them (perhaps most of them) were corrupted by sin. The experience of heaven will involve the redemptive restoration of those forms of enjoyment, and the removal of their evil corruption at the Ultimate Level. This implies that nothing exists here on earth that we consider precious and valuable for which we will not find its infinite substitute in heaven. Life in heaven will be a restoration of every good thing that God intended for us to have when he created us, but which we also lost when we rebelled in the garden. Hence the question of boredom or dullness will certainly not be included in our eternal vocabulary.

From all these considerations, we are left to conclude that heaven is a place that no one should miss. It is a place filled with the promise of seeing our eternal and loving Triune God, who will in every way restore our lives in a way never before anticipated or imagined. When the author of the book of Revelation caught a glimpse of heaven, he was so awestruck with what he saw that he fell down and began to worship the angel that was sent to reveal these eternal truths to him. The angel promptly forbade him, pointing him to the importance of worshiping God rather than God's creation. When he finally completed documenting the revelations presented to him he said, "Amen, come Lord Jesus." The revelation inspired great hope in him of the return of our Lord Jesus Christ. What he saw was so beautiful, elegant and praiseworthy that he had to beseech the Lord Jesus Christ to come. I believe that we would feel the same way if we should ever get a glimpse of heaven. Having thought through this very topic of heaven in this book, though in a severely limited way, I find myself in a spirit of prayer, and it is with just this prayer that I end this book: Come, Lord Jesus!